Child Rhymes & Farm Rhymes by James Whitcomb Riley

Poet and author James Whitcomb Riley was born on October 7th 1849 in Greenfield, Indiana. Better known as the "Hoosier Poet" for his work with regional dialects, and also as the "Children's Poet" Riley was born into an influential and well off family.

However his education was spotty but he was surrounded by creativity which was to stand him in good stead later in life.

His early career was a series of low paid temporary jobs. After stints as a journalist and billboard proprietor he had the resources to dedicate more of his efforts to writing.

Riley was prone to drink which was to affect his health and later his career but after a slow start and a lot of submissions he began to gain traction first in newspapers and then with the publication of his dialect poems 'Boone County Poems' he came to national recognition. This propelled him to long term contracts to perform on speaking circuits. These were very successful but over the years his star waned.

In 1888 he was too drunk to perform and the ensuing publicity made everything seem very bleak for a while. However he overcame that and managed to re-negotiate his contracts so that he received his rightful share of the income and his wealth thereafter increased very quickly.

A bachelor, Riley seems to have his writings as his only outlet, and although in his public performances he was well received, his publications were becoming seen as banal and repetitive and sales of these later works began to fall away.

Eventually after his last tour in 1895 he retired to spend his final years in Indianapolis writing patriotic poetry.

Now in poor health, weakened by years of heavy drinking, Riley, the Hoosier Poet died on July 23, 1916 of a stroke. In a final, unusual tribute, Riley lay in state for a day in the Indiana Statehouse, where thousands came to pay their respects. Not since Lincoln had a public personage received such a send-off. He is buried at Crown Hill Cemetery in Indianapolis.

WITH HALE AFFECTION AND ABIDING FAITH
THESE RHYMES AND PICTURES
ARE INSCRIBED
TO THE CHILDREN EVERYWHERE

He owns the bird-songs of the hills
The laughter of the April rills;
And his are all the diamonds set
In Morning's dewy coronet,
And his the Dusk's first minted stars
That twinkle through the pasture-bars
And litter all the skies at night
With glittering scraps of silver light;
The rainbow's bar, from rim to rim,
In beaten gold, belongs to him.

Index Of Poems

CHILD RHYMES
LITTLE ORPHANT ANNIE
THE RAGGEDY MAN
CURLY LOCKS
THE FUNNY LITTLE FELLOW
THE HAPPY LITTLE CRIPPLE
THE RIDER OF THE KNEE
DOWN AROUND THE RIVER
AT AUNTY'S HOUSE
THE DAYS GONE BY
THE BUMBLEBEE
THE BOY LIVES ON OUR FARM
THE SQUIRTGUN UNCLE MAKED ME
THE OLD TRAMP
OLD AUNT MARY'S
WINTER FANCIES
THE RUNAWAY BOY
THE LITTLE COAT
AN IMPETUOUS RESOLVE
WHO SANTY-CLAUS WUZ
THE NINE LITTLE GOBLINS
TIME OF CLEARER TWITTERINGS
THE CIRCUS-DAY PARADE
THE LUGUBRIOUS WHING-WHANG
WAITIN' FER THE CAT TO DIE
NAUGHTY CLAUDE
THE SOUTH WIND AND THE SUN
THE JOLLY MILLER
OUR HIRED GIRL
THE BOYS' CANDIDATE
THE PET COON
THE OLD HAY-MOW
ON THE SUNNY SIDE
A SUDDEN SHOWER
GRANDFATHER SQUEERS
THE PIXY PEOPLE
A LIFE-LESSON
A HOME-MADE FAIRY-TALE
THE BEAR STORY
ENVOY

FARM RHYMES
TO THE GOOD OLD-FASHIONED PEOPLE
THE ORCHARD LANDS OF LONG AGO
WHEN THE FROST IS ON THE PUNKIN
WHEN THE GREEN GITS BACK IN THE TREES
WET-WEATHER TALK
THE BROOK-SONG

THOUGHTS FER THE DISCURAGED FARMER
"MYLO JONES'S WIFE"
HOW JOHN QUIT THE FARM
A CANARY AT THE FARM
WHERE THE CHILDREN USED TO PLAY
GRIGGSBY'S STATION
KNEE-DEEP IN JUNE
SEPTEMBER DARK
THE CLOVER
OLD OCTOBER
OLD-FASHIONED ROSES
A COUNTRY PATHWAY
WORTERMELON TIME
UP AND DOWN OLD BRANDYWINE
WHEN EARLY MARCH SEEMS MIDDLE MAY
A TALE OF THE AIRLY DAYS
OLD MAN'S NURSERY RHYME
JUNE
THE TREE-TOAD
A SONG OF LONG AGO
OLD WINTERS ON THE FARM
ROMANCIN'

James Whitcomb Riley – A Short Biography

LITTLE ORPHANT ANNIE

Little Orphant Annie's come to our house to stay,
An' wash the cups an' saucers up, an' brush the crumbs away,
An' shoo the chickens off the porch, an' dust the hearth, an' sweep,
An' make the fire, an' bake the bread, an' earn her board-an'-keep;
An' all us other childern, when the supper things is done,
We set around the kitchen fire an' has the mostest fun
A-list'nin' to the witch-tales 'at Annie tells about,
An' the Gobble-uns 'at gits you
Ef you
Don't
Watch
Out!

Onc't they was a little boy wouldn't say his prayers,
So when he went to bed at night, away up stairs,
His Mammy heerd him holler, an' his Daddy heerd him bawl,
An' when they turn't the kivvers down, he wasn't there at all!
An' they seeked him in the rafter-room, an' cubby-hole, an' press,
An' seeked him up the chimbly-flue, an' ever'wheres, I guess;
But all they ever found was thist his pants an' roundabout:
An' the Gobble-uns'll git you
Ef you
Don't

Watch
Out!

An' one time a little girl 'ud allus laugh an' grin,
An' make fun of ever'one, an' all her blood an' kin;
An' onc't, when they was "company," an' ole folks was there,
She mocked 'em an' shocked 'em, an' said she didn't care!
An' thist as she kicked her heels, an' turn't to run an' hide,
They was two great big Black Things a-standin' by her side,
An' they snatched her through the ceilin' 'fore she knowed what she's about!
An' the Gobble-uns'll git you
Ef you
Don't
Watch
Out!

An' little Orphant Annie says when the blaze is blue,
An' the lamp-wick sputters, an' the wind goes woo-oo!
An' you hear the crickets quit, an' the moon is gray,
An' the lightnin'-bugs in dew is all squenched away,
You better mind yer parents, an' yer teachers fond an' dear,
An' churish them 'at loves you, an' dry the orphant's tear,
An' he'p the pore an' needy ones 'at clusters all about,
Er the Gobble-uns'll git you
Ef you
Don't
Watch
Out!

THE RAGGEDY MAN

O The Raggedy Man! He works fer Pa;
An' he's the goodest man ever you saw!
He comes to our house every day,
An' waters the horses, an' feeds 'em hay;
An' he opens the shed an' we all ist laugh
When he drives out our little old wobble-ly calf;
An' nen ef our hired girl says he can
He milks the cow fer 'Lizabuth Ann.
Aint he a' awful good Raggedy Man?
Raggedy! Raggedy! Raggedy Man!

W'y, The Raggedy Man he's ist so good
He splits the kindlin' an' chops the wood;
An' nen he spades in our garden, too,
An' does most things 'at boys can't do!
He clumbed clean up in our big tree
An' shooked a' apple down fer me
An' nother'n', too, fer 'Lizabuth Ann
An' nother'n', too, fer The Raggedy Man.

Aint he a' awful kind Raggedy Man?
Raggedy! Raggedy! Raggedy Man!

An' The Raggedy Man, he knows most rhymes
An' tells 'em, ef I be good, sometimes:
Knows 'bout Giunts, an' Griffuns, an' Elves,
An' the Squidgicum-Squees 'at swallers therselves!
An', wite by the pump in our pasture-lot,
He showed me the hole 'at the Wunks is got,
'At lives 'way deep in the ground, an' can
Turn into me, er 'Lizabuth Ann!
Aint he a funny old Raggedy Man?
Raggedy! Raggedy! Raggedy Man!

The Raggedy Man, one time when he
Wuz makin' a little bow-'n'-orry fer me,
Says "When you're big like your Pa is,
Air you go' to keep a fine store like his
An' be a rich merchunt an' wear fine clothes?
Er what air you go' to be, goodness knows!"
An' nen he laughed at 'Lizabuth Ann,
An' I says "'M go' to be a Raggedy Man!
I'm ist go' to be a nice Raggedy Man!"
Raggedy! Raggedy! Raggedy Man!

CURLY LOCKS

Curly Locks! Curly Locks! wilt thou be mine?
Thou shalt not wash the dishes, nor yet feed the swine,
But sit on a cushion and sew a fine seam,
And feast upon strawberries, sugar and cream.

Curly Locks! Curly Locks! wilt thou be mine?
The throb of my heart is in every line,
And the pulse of a passion as airy and glad
In its musical beat as the little Prince had!

Thou shalt not wash the dishes, nor yet feed the swine!
O I'll dapple thy hands with these kisses of mine
Till the pink of the nail of each finger shall be
As a little pet blush in full blossom for me.

But sit on a cushion and sew a fine seam,
And thou shalt have fabric as fair as a dream,
The red of my veins, and the white of my love,
And the gold of my joy for the braiding thereof.

And feast upon strawberries, sugar and cream
From a service of silver, with jewels agleam,
At thy feet will I bide, at thy beck will I rise,

And twinkle my soul in the night of thine eyes!

Curly Locks! Curly Locks! wilt thou be mine?
Thou shalt not wash the dishes, nor yet feed the swine.
But sit on a cushion and sew a fine seam,
And feast upon strawberries, sugar and cream.

THE FUNNY LITTLE FELLOW
'Twas a Funny Little Fellow
Of the very purest type,
For he had a heart as mellow
As an apple over-ripe;
And the brightest little twinkle
When a funny thing occurred,
And the lightest little tinkle
Of a laugh you ever heard!

His smile was like the glitter
Of the sun in tropic lands,
And his talk a sweeter twitter
Than the swallow understands;
Hear him sing and tell a story
Snap a joke, ignite a pun,
'Twas a capture, rapture, glory,
And explosion, all in one!

Though he hadn't any money
That condiment which tends
To make a fellow "honey"
For the palate of his friends;
Sweet simples he compounded
Sovereign antidotes for sin
Or taint, a faith unbounded
That his friends were genuine.

He wasn't honored, may be
For his songs of praise were slim,
Yet I never knew a baby
That wouldn't crow for him;
I never knew a mother
But urged a kindly claim
Upon him as a brother,
At the mention of his name.

The sick have ceased their sighing
And have even found the grace
Of a smile when they were dying
As they looked upon his face;
And I've seen his eyes of laughter

Melt in tears that only ran
As though, swift dancing after,
Came the Funny Little Man.

He laughed away the sorrow,
And he laughed away the gloom
We are all so prone to borrow
From the darkness of the tomb;
And he laughed across the ocean
Of a happy life, and passed,
With a laugh of glad emotion,
Into Paradise at last.

And I think the Angels knew him,
And had gathered to await
His coming, and run to him
Through the widely-opened Gate
With their faces gleaming sunny
For his laughter-loving sake,
And thinking, "What a funny
Little Angel he will make!"

THE HAPPY LITTLE CRIPPLE

I'm thist a little cripple boy, an' never goin' to grow
An' get a great big man at all! 'cause Aunty told me so.
When I was thist a baby onc't, I falled out of the bed
An' got "The Curv'ture of the Spine" 'at's what the Doctor said.
I never had no Mother nen, fer my Pa runned away
An' dassn't come back here no more, 'cause he was drunk one day
An' stobbed a man in thish-ere town, an' couldn't pay his fine!
An' nen my Ma she died an' I got "Curv'ture of the Spine!"

I'm nine years old! An' you can't guess how much I weigh, I bet!
Last birthday I weighed thirty-three! An' I weigh thirty yet!
I'm awful little fer my size I'm purt' nigh littler 'nan
Some babies is! an' neighbors all calls me "The Little Man!"
An' Doc one time he laughed an' said: "I 'spect, first thing you know,
You'll have a little spike-tail coat an' travel with a show!"
An' nen I laughed, till I looked round an' Aunty was a-cryin'
Sometimes she acts like that, 'cause I got "Curv'ture of the Spine."

I set, while Aunty's washin', on my little long-leg stool,
An' watch the little boys an' girls a-skippin' by to school;
An' I peck on the winder, an' holler out an' say:
"Who wants to fight The Little Man 'at dares you all today?"
An', nen the boys climbs on the fence, an' little girls peeks through,
An' they all says: "Cause you're so big, you think we're 'feared o' you!"
An' nen they yell, an' shake their fist at me, like I shake mine
They're thist in fun, you know, 'cause I got "Curv'ture of the Spine!"

At evening, when the ironin's done, an' Aunty's fixed the fire,
An' filled an' lit the lamp, an' trimmed the wick an' turned it higher,
An' fetched the wood all in fer night, an' locked the kitchen door,
An' stuffed the ole crack where the wind blows in up through the floor
She sets the kittle on the coals, an' biles an' makes the tea,
An' fries the liver an' the mush, an' cooks a egg fer me;
An' sometimes, when I cough so hard, her elderberry wine
Don't go so bad fer little boys with "Curv'ture of the Spine!"

But Aunty's all so childish-like on my account, you see,
I'm 'most afeard she'll be took down an' 'at's what bothers me!
'Cause ef my good old Aunty ever would git sick an' die,
I don't know what she'd do in heaven, till I come, by an' by:
Fer she's so ust to all my ways, an' ever'thing, you know,
An' no one there like me, to nuss an' worry over so!
'Cause all the little childerns there's so straight an' strong an' fine,
They's nary angel 'bout the place with "Curv'ture of the Spine!"

THE RIDER OF THE KNEE
Knightly Rider of the Knee
Of Proud-prancing Unclery!
Gaily mount, and wave the sign
Of that mastery of thine.

Pat thy steed and turn him free,
Knightly Rider of the Knee!
Sit thy charger as a throne
Lash him with thy laugh alone:

Sting him only with the spur
Of such wit as may occur,
Knightly Rider of the Knee,
In thy shriek of ecstasy.

Would, as now, we might endure,
Twain as one, thou miniature
Ruler, at the rein of me
Knightly Rider of the Knee!

DOWN AROUND THE RIVER
Noon-time an' June-time, down around the river!
Have to furse with 'Lizey Ann but lawzy! I fergive her!
Drives me off the place, an' says 'at all 'at she's a-wishin',
Land o' gracious! time'll come I'll git enough o' fishin'!
Little Dave, a-choppin' wood, never 'pears to notice;
Don't know where she's hid his hat, er keerin' where his coat is,

Specalatin', more'n like, he haint a-goin' to mind me,
An' guessin' where, say twelve o'clock, a feller'd likely find me!

Noon-time an' June-time, down around the river!
Clean out o' sight o' home, an' skulkin' under kivver
Of the sycamores, jack-oaks, an' swamp-ash an' ellum
Idies all so jumbled up, you kin hardly tell 'em!
Tired, you know, but lovin' it, an' smilin' jes' to think 'at
Any sweeter tiredness you'd fairly want to drink it!
Tired o' fishin', tired o' fun, line out slack an' slacker
All you want in all the world's a little more tobacker!

Hungry, but a-hidin' it, er jes' a-not a-keerin':
Kingfisher gittin' up an' skootin' out o' hearin';
Snipes on the t'other side, where the County Ditch is,
Wadin' up an' down the aidge like they'd rolled their britches!
Old turkle on the root kindo-sorto drappin'
Intoo th' worter like he don't know how it happen!
Worter, shade an' all so mixed, don't know which you'd orter
Say; th' worter in the shadder, shadder in the worter!

Somebody hollerin', 'way around the bend in
Upper Fork, where yer eye kin jes' ketch the endin'
Of the shiney wedge o' wake some muss-rat's a-makin'
With that pesky nose o' his! Then a sniff o' bacon,
Corn-bred an' 'dock-greens an' little Dave a-shinnin'
'Crost the rocks an' mussel-shells, a-limpin' an' a-grinnin',
With yer dinner fer ye, an' a blessin' from the giver,
Noon-time an' June-time down around the river!

AT AUNTY'S HOUSE

One time, when we'z at Aunty's house
'Way in the country! where
They's ist but woods an' pigs, an' cows
An' all's out-doors an' air!
An' orchurd-swing; an' churry-trees
An' churries in 'em! Yes, an' these
Here red-head birds steals all they please,
An' tetch 'em ef you dare!
W'y, wunst, one time, when we wuz there,
We et out on the porch!

Wite where the cellar-door wuz shut
The table wuz; an' I
Let Aunty set by me an' cut
My vittuls up an' pie.
'Tuz awful funny! I could see
The red-heads in the churry-tree;
An' bee-hives, where you got to be

So keerful, goin' by;
An' "Comp'ny" there an' all! an' we
We et out on the porch!

An' I ist et p'surves an' things
'At Ma don't 'low me to
An' chickun-gizzurds (don't like wings
Like Parunts does! do you?)
An' all the time, the wind blowed there,
An' I could feel it in my hair,
An' ist smell clover ever'where!
An' a' old red-head flew
Purt' nigh wite over my high-chair,
When we et on the porch!

THE DAYS GONE BY

O the days gone by! O the days gone by!
The apples in the orchard, and the pathway through the rye;
The chirrup of the robin, and the whistle of the quail
As he piped across the meadows sweet as any nightingale;
When the bloom was on the clover, and the blue was in the sky,
And my happy heart brimmed over, in the days gone by.

In the days gone by, when my naked feet were tripped
By the honeysuckle tangles where the water-lilies dipped,
And the ripples of the river lipped the moss along the brink,
Where the placid-eyed and lazy-footed cattle came to drink,
And the tilting snipe stood fearless of the truant's wayward cry
And the splashing of the swimmer, in the days gone by.

O the days gone by! O the days gone by!
The music of the laughing lip, the lustre of the eye;
The childish faith in fairies, and Aladdin's magic ring
The simple, soul-reposing, glad belief in everything,
When life was like a story, holding neither sob nor sigh,
In the golden olden glory of the days gone by.

THE BUMBLEBEE

You better not fool with a Bumblebee!
Ef you don't think they can sting you'll see!
They're lazy to look at, an' kindo' go
Buzzin' an' bummin' aroun' so slow,
An' ac' so slouchy an' all fagged out,
Danglin' their legs as they drone about
The hollyhawks 'at they can't climb in
'Ithout ist a-tumble-un out agin!
Wunst I watched one climb clean 'way

In a jim'son-blossom, I did, one day,
An' I ist grabbed it an' nen let go
An' "Ooh-ooh! Honey! I told ye so!"
Says The Raggedy Man; an' he ist run
An' pullt out the stinger, an' don't laugh none,
An' says: "They has ben folks, I guess,
'At thought I wuz predjudust, more er less,
Yit I still muntain 'at a Bumblebee
Wears out his welcome too quick fer me!"

THE BOY LIVES ON OUR FARM
The boy lives on our Farm, he's not
Afeard o' horses none!
An' he can make 'em lope, er trot,
Er rack, er pace, er run.
Sometimes he drives two horses, when
He comes to town an' brings
A wagon-full o' 'taters nen,
An' roastin'-ears an' things.

Two horses is "a team," he says,
An' when you drive er hitch,
The right-un's a "near-horse," I guess
Er "off" I don't know which
The Boy lives on our Farm, he told
Me, too, 'at he can see,
By lookin' at their teeth, how old
A horse is, to a T!

I'd be the gladdest boy alive
Ef I knowed much as that,
An' could stand up like him an' drive,
An' ist push back my hat,
Like he comes skallyhootin' through
Our alley, with one arm
A-wavin' Fare-ye-well! to you
The Boy lives on our Farm!

THE SQUIRTGUN UNCLE MAKED ME
Uncle Sidney, when he wuz here,
Maked me a squirtgun out o' some
Elder-bushes 'at growed out near
Where wuz the brickyard, 'way out clear
To where the toll-gate come!

So when we walked back home again,
He maked it, out in our woodhouse where

Wuz the old workbench, an' the old jack-plane,
An' the old 'pokeshave, an' the tools all lay'n'
Ist like he wants 'em there.

He sawed it first with the old hand-saw;
An' nen he peeled off the bark, an' got
Some glass an' scraped it; an' told 'bout Pa,
When he wuz a boy an' fooled his Ma,
An' the whippin' 'at he caught.

Nen Uncle Sidney, he took an' filed
A' old arn ramrod; an' one o' the ends
He screwed fast into the vise; an' smiled,
Thinkin', he said, o' when he wuz a child,
'Fore him an' Pa wuz mens.

He punched out the peth, an' nen he put
A plug in the end with a hole notched through;
Nen took the old drawey-knife an' cut
An' maked a handle 'at shoved clean shut
But ist where yer hand held to.

An' he wropt th'uther end with some string an' white
Piece o' the sleeve of a' old tored shirt;
An' nen he showed me to hold it tight,
An' suck in the water an' work it right
An' it 'ud ist squirt an' squirt!

THE OLD TRAMP

A Old Tramp slep' in our stable wunst,
An' The Raggedy Man he caught
An' roust him up, an' chased him off
Clean out through our back lot!

An' th' Old Tramp hollered back an' said,
"You're a purty man! You air!
With a pair o' eyes like two fried eggs,
An' a nose like a Bartlutt pear!"

OLD AUNT MARY'S

Wasn't it pleasant, O brother mine,
In those old days of the lost sunshine
Of youth when the Saturday's chores were through,
And the "Sunday's wood" in the kitchen, too,
And we went visiting, "me and you,"
Out to Old Aunt Mary's?

It all comes back so clear to-day!
Though I am as bald as you are gray
Out by the barn-lot, and down the lane,
We patter along in the dust again,
As light as the tips of the drops of the rain,
Out to Old Aunt Mary's!

We cross the pasture, and through the wood
Where the old gray snag of the poplar stood,
Where the hammering "red-heads" hopped awry,
And the buzzard "raised" in the "clearing" sky
And lolled and circled, as we went by
Out to Old Aunt Mary's.

And then in the dust of the road again;
And the teams we met, and the countrymen;
And the long highway, with sunshine spread
As thick as butter on country bread,
Our cares behind, and our hearts ahead
Out to Old Aunt Mary's.

Why, I see her now in the open door,
Where the little gourds grew up the sides and o'er
The clapboard roof! And her face ah, me!
Wasn't it good for a boy to see
And wasn't it good for a boy to be
Out to Old Aunt Mary's?

And O my brother, so far away,
This is to tell you she waits to-day
To welcome us: Aunt Mary fell
Asleep this morning, whispering, "Tell
The boys to come!" And all is well
Out to Old Aunt Mary's.

WINTER FANCIES
I
Winter without
And warmth within;
The winds may shout
And the storm begin;
The snows may pack
At the window pane,
And the skies grow black,
And the sun remain
Hidden away
The livelong day
But here in here is the warmth of May!

II

Swoop your spitefullest
Up the flue,
Wild Winds do!
What in the world do I care for you?
O delightfullest
Weather of all,
Howl and squall,
And shake the trees till the last leaves fall!

III

The joy one feels,
In an easy chair,
Cocking his heels
In the dancing air
That wreathes the rim of a roaring stove
Whose heat loves better than hearts can love,
Will not permit
The coldest day
To drive away
The fire in his blood, and the bliss of it!

IV

Then blow, Winds, blow!
And rave and shriek,
And snarl and snow
Till your breath grows weak
While here in my room
I'm as snugly shut
As a glad little worm
In the heart of a nut!

THE RUNAWAY BOY

Wunst I sassed my Pa, an' he
Won't stand that, an' punished me,
Nen when he was gone that day,
I slipped out an' runned away.

I tooked all my copper-cents,
An' clumbed over our back fence
In the jimpson-weeds 'at growed
Ever'where all down the road.

Nen I got out there, an' nen
I runned some an' runned again
When I met a man 'at led
A big cow 'at shooked her head.

I went down a long, long lane

Where was little pigs a-play'n';
An' a grea'-big pig went "Booh!"
An' jumped up, an' skeered me too.

Nen I scampered past, an' they
Was somebody hollered "Hey!"
An' I ist looked ever'where,
An' they was nobody there.

I Want to, but I'm 'fraid to try
To go back.... An' by-an'-by
Somepin' hurts my throat inside
An' I want my Ma an' cried.

Nen a grea'-big girl come through
Where's a gate, an' telled me who
Am I? an' ef I tell where
My home's at she'll show me there.

But I couldn't ist but tell
What's my name; an' she says well,
An' she tooked me up an' says
She know where I live, she guess.

Nen she telled me hug wite close
Round her neck! an' off she goes
Skippin' up the street! An' nen
Purty soon I'm home again.

An' my Ma, when she kissed me,
Kissed the big girl too, an' she
Kissed me ef I p'omise shore
I won't run away no more!

THE LITTLE COAT
Here's his ragged "roundabout";
Turn the pockets inside out:
See; his pen-knife, lost to use,
Rusted shut with apple-juice;
Here, with marbles, top and string,
Is his deadly "devil-sling,"
With its rubber, limp at last
As the sparrows of the past!
Beeswax, buckles, leather straps
Bullets, and a box of caps,
Not a thing of all, I guess,
But betrays some waywardness
E'en these tickets, blue and red,
For the Bible-verses said

Such as this his mem'ry kept
"Jesus wept."

Here's a fishing hook-and-line,
Tangled up with wire and twine,
And dead angle-worms, and some
Slugs of lead and chewing-gum,
Blent with scents that can but come
From the oil of rhodium.
Here a soiled, yet dainty note,
That some little sweetheart wrote,
Dotting, "Vine grows round the stump,"
And "My sweetest sugar lump!"
Wrapped in this a padlock key
Where he's filed a touch-hole see!
And some powder in a quill
Corked up with a liver pill;
And a spongy little chunk
Of "punk."

Here's the little coat but O!
Where is he we've censured so!
Don't you hear us calling, dear?
Back! come back, and never fear.
You may wander where you will,
Over orchard, field and hill;
You may kill the birds, or do
Anything that pleases you!
Ah, this empty coat of his!
Every tatter worth a kiss;
Every stain as pure instead
As the white stars overhead:
And the pockets, homes were they
Of the little hands that play
Now no more but, absent, thus
Beckon us.

AN IMPETUOUS RESOLVE
When little Dickie Swope's a man,
He's go' to be a Sailor;
An' little Hamey Tincher, he's
A-go' to be a Tailor:
Bud Mitchell, he's a-go' to be
A stylish Carriage-Maker;
An' when I grow a grea'-big man,
I'm go' to be a Baker!

An' Dick'll buy his sailor-suit
O' Hame; and Hame'll take it
An' buy as fine a double-rigg

As ever Bud can make it:
An' nen all three'll drive roun' fer me
An' we'll drive off togevver,
A-slingin' pie-crust 'long the road
Ferever an' ferever!

WHO SANTY-CLAUS WUZ

Jes' a little bit o' feller, I remember still
Ust to almost cry fer Christmas, like a youngster will.
Fourth o' July's nothin' to it! New Year's ain't a smell!
Easter-Sunday, Circus-day, jes' all dead in the shell!
Lawzy, though! at night, you know, to set around an' hear
The old folks work the story off about the sledge an' deer,
An' "Santy" skootin' round the roof, all wrapt in fur an' fuzz
Long afore
I knowed who
"Santy-Claus" wuz!

Ust to wait, an' set up late, a week er two ahead;
Couldn't hardly keep awake, ner wouldn't go to bed;
Kittle stewin' on the fire, an' Mother settin' here
Darnin' socks, an' rockin' in the skreeky rockin'-cheer;
Pap gap', an' wonder where it wuz the money went,
An' quar'l with his frosted heels, an' spill his liniment;
An' me a-dreamin' sleigh-bells when the clock 'ud whir an' buzz,
Long afore
I knowed who
"Santy-Claus" wuz!

Size the fire-place up an' figger how "Ole Santy" could
Manage to come down the chimbly, like they said he would;
Wisht 'at I could hide an' see him, wunderd what he'd say
Ef he ketched a feller layin' fer him thataway!
But I bet on him, an' liked him, same as ef he had
Turned to pat me on the back an' say, "Look here, my lad,
Here's my pack, jes' he'p yourse'f, like all good boys does!"
Long afore
I knowed who
"Santy-Claus" wuz!

Wisht that yarn was true about him, as it 'peared to be
Truth made out o' lies like that-un's good enough fer me!
Wisht I still wuz so confidin' I could jes' go wild
Over hangin' up my stockin's, like the little child
Climbin' in my lap to-night, an' beggin' me to tell
'Bout them reindeers, and "Old Santy" that she loves so well
I'm half sorry fer this little-girl-sweetheart of his
Long afore
She knows who

"Santy-Claus" is!

THE NINE LITTLE GOBLINS

They all climbed up on a high board-fence
Nine little Goblins, with green-glass eyes
Nine little Goblins that had no sense,
And couldn't tell coppers from cold mince pies;
And they all climbed up on the fence, and sat
And I asked them what they were staring at.

And the first one said, as he scratched his head
With a queer little arm that reached out of his ear
And rasped its claws in his hair so red
"This is what this little arm is fer!"
And he scratched and stared, and the next one said,
"How on earth do you scratch your head?"

And he laughed like the screech of a rusty hinge
Laughed and laughed till his face grew black;
And when he choked, with a final twinge
Of his stifling laughter, he thumped his back
With a fist that grew on the end of his tail
Till the breath came back to his lips so pale.

And the third little Goblin leered round at me
And there were no lids on his eyes at all
And he clucked one eye, and he says, says he,
"What is the style of your socks this fall?"
And he clapped his heels and I sighed to see
That he had hands where his feet should be.

Then a bald-faced Goblin, gray and grim,
Bowed his head, and I saw him slip
His eyebrows off, as I looked at him,
And paste them over his upper lip;
And then he moaned in remorseful pain
"Would - Ah, would I'd me brows again!"

And then the whole of the Goblin band
Rocked on the fence-top to and fro,
And clung, in a long row, hand in hand,
Singing the songs that they used to know
Singing the songs that their grandsires sung
In the goo-goo days of the Goblin-tongue.

And ever they kept their green-glass eyes
Fixed on me with a stony stare
Till my own grew glazed with a dread surmise,
And my hat whooped up on my lifted hair,

And I felt the heart in my breast snap to
As you've heard the lid of a snuff-box do.

And they sang "You're asleep! There is no board-fence,
And never a Goblin with green-glass eyes!
'Tis only a vision the mind invents
After a supper of cold mince-pies,
And you're doomed to dream this way," they said,
"And you sha'n't wake up till you're clean plum dead!"

TIME OF CLEARER TWITTERINGS
I.
Time of crisp and tawny leaves,
And of tarnished harvest sheaves,
And of dusty grasses, weeds
Thistles, with their tufted seeds
Voyaging the Autumn breeze
Like as fairy argosies:
Time of quicker flash of wings,
And of clearer twitterings
In the grove, or deeper shade
Of the tangled everglade,
Where the spotted water-snake
Coils him in the sunniest brake;
And the bittern, as in fright,
Darts, in sudden, slanting flight,
Southward, while the startled crane
Films his eyes in dreams again.

II
Down along the dwindled creek
We go loitering. We speak
Only with old questionings
Of the dear remembered things
Of the days of long ago,
When the stream seemed thus and so
In our boyish eyes: The bank
Greener then, through rank on rank
Of the mottled sycamores,
Touching tops across the shores:
Here, the hazel thicket stood
There, the almost pathless wood
Where the shellbark hickory tree
Rained its wealth on you and me.
Autumn! as you loved us then,
Take us to your heart again!

III
Season halest of the year!

How the zestful atmosphere
Nettles blood and brain, and smites
Into life the old delights
We have tasted in our youth,
And our graver years, forsooth!
How again the boyish heart
Leaps to see the chipmunk start
From the brush and sleek the sun
Very beauty, as he runs!
How again a subtle hint
Of crushed pennyroyal or mint,
Sends us on our knees, as when
We were truant boys of ten
Brown marauders of the wood,
Merrier than Robin Hood!

IV

Ah! will any minstrel say,
In his sweetest roundelay,
What is sweeter, after all,
Than black haws, in early Fall
Fruit so sweet the frost first sat,
Dainty-toothed, and nibbled at!
And will any poet sing
Of a lusher, richer thing
Than a ripe May-apple, rolled
Like a pulpy lump of gold
Under thumb and finger-tips,
And poured molten through the lips?
Go, ye bards of classic themes,
Pipe your songs by classic streams!
I would twang the redbird's wings
In the thicket while he sings!

THE CIRCUS-DAY PARADE

Oh, the Circus-Day parade! How the bugles played and played!
And how the glossy horses tossed their flossy manes, and neighed,
As the rattle and the rhyme of the tenor-drummer's time
Filled all the hungry hearts of us with melody sublime!

How the grand band-wagon shone with a splendor all its own,
And glittered with a glory that our dreams had never known!
And how the boys behind, high and low of every kind,
Marched in unconscious capture, with a rapture undefined!

How the horsemen, two and two, with their plumes of white and blue,
And crimson, gold and purple, nodding by at me and you.
Waved the banners that they bore, as the Knights in days of yore,
Till our glad eyes gleamed and glistened like the spangles that they wore!

How the graceless-graceful stride of the elephant was eyed,
And the capers of the little horse that cantered at his side!
How the shambling camels, tame to the plaudits of their fame,
With listless eyes came silent, masticating as they came.

How the cages jolted past, with each wagon battened fast,
And the mystery within it only hinted of at last
From the little grated square in the rear, and nosing there
The snout of some strange animal that sniffed the outer air!

And, last of all, The Clown, making mirth for all the town,
With his lips curved ever upward and his eyebrows ever down,
And his chief attention paid to the little mule that played
A tattoo on the dashboard with his heels, in the parade.

Oh! the Circus-Day parade! How the bugles played and played!
And how the glossy horses tossed their flossy manes and neighed.
As the rattle and the rhyme of the tenor-drummer's time
Filled all the hungry hearts of us with melody sublime!

THE LUGUBRIOUS WHING-WHANG
The rhyme o' The Raggedy Man's 'at's best
Is Tickle me, Love, in these Lonesome Ribs,
'Cause that-un's the strangest of all o' the rest,
An' the worst to learn, an' the last one guessed,
An' the funniest one, an' the foolishest.
Tickle me, Love, in these Lonesome Ribs!

I don't know what in the world it means
Tickle me, Love, in these Lonesome Ribs!
An' nen when I tell him I don't, he leans
Like he was a-grindin' on some machines
An' says: Ef I don't, w'y, I don't know beans!
Tickle me, Love, in these Lonesome Ribs!

Out on the margin of Moonshine Land,
Tickle me, Love, in these Lonesome Ribs!
Out where the Whing-Whang loves to stand,
Writing his name with his tail in the sand,
And swiping it out with his oogerish hand;
Tickle me, Love, in these Lonesome Ribs!

Is it the gibber of Gungs or Keeks?
Tickle me, Love, in these Lonesome Ribs!
Or what is the sound that the Whing-Whang seeks?
Crouching low by the winding creeks
And holding his breath for weeks and weeks!
Tickle me, Love, in these Lonesome Ribs!

Aroint him the wraithest of wraithly things!
Tickle me, Love, in these Lonesome Ribs!
'Tis a fair Whing-Whangess, with phosphor rings
And bridal-jewels of fangs and stings;
And she sits and as sadly and softly sings
As the mildewed whir of her own dead wings,
Tickle me, Dear,
Tickle me here,
Tickle me, Love, in these Lonesome Ribs!

WAITIN' FER THE CAT TO DIE
Lawzy! don't I rickollect
That-'air old swing in the lane!
Right and proper, I expect,
Old times can't come back again;
But I want to state, ef they
Could come back, and I could say
What my pick 'ud be, i jing!
I'd say, Gimme the old swing
'Nunder the old locus'-trees
On the old place, ef you please!
Danglin' there with half-shet eye,
Waitin' fer the cat to die!

I'd say, Gimme the old gang
Of barefooted, hungry, lean,
Ornry boys you want to hang
When you're growed up twic't as mean!
The old gyarden-patch, the old
Truants, and the stuff we stol'd!
The old stompin'-groun', where we
Wore the grass off, wild and free
As the swoop of the old swing,
Where we ust to climb and cling,
And twist roun', and fight, and lie
Waitin' fer the cat to die!

'Pears like I 'most allus could
Swing the highest of the crowd
Jes sail up there tel I stood
Downside-up, and screech out loud,
Ketch my breath, and jes drap back
Fer to let the old swing slack,
Yit my tow-head dippin' still
In the green boughs, and the chill
Up my backbone taperin' down,
With my shadder on the ground'

Slow and slower trailin' by
Waitin' fer the cat to die!

Now my daughter's little Jane's
Got a kind o' baby-swing
On the porch, so's when it rains
She kin play there little thing!
And I'd limped out t'other day
With my old cheer this-a-way,
Swingin' her and rockin' too,
Thinkin' how I ust to do
At her age, when suddently,
"Hey, Gran'pap!" she says to me,
"Why you rock so slow?" ... Says I,
"Waitin' fer the cat to die!"

NAUGHTY CLAUDE

When Little Claude was naughty wunst
At dinner-time, an' said
He won't say "Thank you" to his Ma,
She maked him go to bed
An' stay two hours an' not git up,
So when the clock struck Two,
Nen Claude says, "Thank you, Mr. Clock,
I'm much obleeged to you!"

THE SOUTH WIND AND THE SUN

O the South Wind and the Sun
How each loved the other one
Full of fancy, full of folly
Full of jollity and fun!
How they romped and ran about,
Like two boys when school is out,
With glowing face, and lisping lip,
Low laugh, and lifted shout!

And the South Wind he was dressed
With a ribbon round his breast
That floated, flapped and fluttered
In a riotous unrest;
And a drapery of mist,
From the shoulder and the wrist
Flowing backward with the motion
Of the waving hand he kissed.

And the Sun had on a crown
Wrought of gilded thistledown,

And a scarf of velvet vapor,
And a raveled-rainbow gown;
And his tinsel-tangled hair,
Tossed and lost upon the air,
With glossier and flossier
Than any anywhere.

And the South Wind's eyes were two
Little dancing drops of dew,
As he puffed his cheeks, and pursed his lips,
And blew and blew and blew!
And the Sun's like diamond-stone,
Brighter yet than ever known,
As he knit his brows and held his breath,
And shone and shone and shone!

And this pair of merry fays
Wandered through the summer days;
Arm-in-arm they went together
Over heights of morning haze
Over slanting slopes of lawn
They went on and on and on,
Where the daisies looked like star-tracks
Trailing up and down the dawn.

And where'er they found the top
Of a wheat-stalk droop and lop,
They chucked it underneath the chin
And praised the lavish crop,
Till it lifted with the pride
Of the heads it grew beside,
And then the South Wind and the Sun
Went onward satisfied.

Over meadow-lands they tripped,
Where the dandelions dipped
In crimson foam of clover bloom
And dripped and dripped and dripped!
And they clinched the bumble-stings,
Gauming honey on their wings,
And bundling them in lily-bells,
With maudlin murmurings.

And the humming-bird, that hung
Like a jewel up among
The tilted honeysuckle horns,
They mesmerized and swung
In the palpitating air,
Drowsed with odors strange and rare,
And, with whispered laughter, slipped away,
And left him hanging there.

And they braided blades of grass
Where the truant had to pass;
And they wriggled through the rushes
And the reeds of the morass,
Where they danced, in rapture sweet,
O'er the leaves that laid a street
Of undulant mosaic for
The touches of their feet.

By the brook with mossy brink,
Where the cattle came to drink,
They trilled and piped and whistled
With the thrush and bobolink,
Till the kine, in listless pause,
Switched their tails in mute applause,
With lifted heads, and dreamy eyes,
And bubble-dripping jaws.

And where the melons grew,
Streaked with yellow, green and blue,
These jolly sprites went wandering
Through spangled paths of dew;
And the melons, here and there,
They made love to, everywhere,
Turning their pink souls to crimson
With caresses fond and fair.

Over orchard walls they went,
Where the fruited boughs were bent
Till they brushed the sward beneath them
Where the shine and shadow blent;
And the great green pear they shook
Till the sallow hue forsook
Its features, and the gleam of gold
Laughed out in every look.

And they stroked the downy cheek
Of the peach, and smoothed it sleek,
And flushed it into splendor;
And, with many an elfish freak,
Gave the russet's rust a wipe
Prankt the rambo with a stripe,
And the winesap blushed its reddest
As they spanked the pippins ripe.

Through the woven ambuscade
That the twining vines had made,
They found the grapes, in clusters,
Drinking up the shine and shade
Plumpt, like tiny skins of wine,

With a vintage so divine
That the tongue of Fancy tingled
With the tang of muscadine.

And the golden-banded bees,
Droning o'er the flowery leas,
They bridled, reined, and rode away
Across the fragrant breeze,
Till in hollow oak and elm
They had groomed and stabled them
In waxen stalls that oozed with dews
Of rose and lily-stem.

Where the dusty highway leads,
High above the wayside weeds,
They sowed the air with butterflies
Like blooming flower-seeds,
Till the dull grasshopper sprung
Half a man's-height up, and hung
Tranced in the heat, with whirring wings,
And sung and sung and sung!

And they loitered, hand in hand,
Where the snipe along the sand
Of the river ran to meet them
As the ripple meets the land,
Till the dragonfly, in light
Gauzy armor, burnished bright,
Came tilting down the waters
In a wild, bewildered flight.

And they heard the kildee's call,
And afar, the waterfall,
But the rustle of a falling leaf
They heard above it all;
And the trailing willow crept
Deeper in the tide that swept
The leafy shallop to the shore,
And wept and wept and wept!

And the fairy vessel veered
From its moorings, tacked and steered
For the center of the current
Sailed away and disappeared:
And the burthen that it bore
From the long-enchanted shore
"Alas! the South Wind and the Sun!"
I murmur evermore.

For the South Wind and the Sun,
Each so loves the other one,

For all his jolly folly,
And frivolity and fun,
That our love for them they weigh
As their fickle fancies may,
And when at last we love them most,
They laugh and sail away.

THE JOLLY MILLER

It was a Jolly Miller lived on the River Dee;
He looked upon his piller, and there he found a flea:
"O Mr. Flea! you have bit' me,
And you shall shorely die!"
So he scrunched his bones against the stones
And there he let him lie!

Twas then the Jolly Miller he laughed and told his wife,
And she laughed fit to kill her, and dropped her carvin'-knife!
"O Mr. Flea!" "Ho-ho!" "Tee-hee!"
They both laughed fit to kill,
Until the sound did almost drownd
The rumble of the mill!

"Laugh on, my Jolly Miller! and Missus Miller, too!
But there's a weeping-willer will soon wave over you!"
The voice was all so awful small
So very small and slim!
He durst' infer that it was her,
Ner her infer 'twas him!

That night the Jolly Miller, says he, "It's Wifey dear,
That cat o' yourn, I'd kill her! her actions is so queer,
She rubbin' 'ginst the grindstone-legs,
And yowlin' at the sky
And I 'low the moon haint greener
Than the yaller of her eye!"

And as the Jolly Miller went chuckle-un to bed,
Was Somepin jerked his piller from underneath his head!
"O Wife," says he, on-easi-lee,
"Fetch here that lantern there!"
But Somepin moans in thunder tones,
"You tetch it ef you dare!"

'Twas then the Jolly Miller he trimbled and he quailed
And his wife choked until her breath come back, 'n' she wailed!
And "O!" cried she, "it is the Flea,
All white and pale and wann
He's got you in his clutches, and
He's bigger than a man!"

"Ho! ho! my Jolly Miller," (fer 'twas the Flea, fer shore!)
"I reckon you'll not rack my bones ner scrunch 'em any more!"
And then the Ghost he grabbed him clos't,
WIth many a ghastly smile,
And from the doorstep stooped and hopped
About four hundred mile!

OUR HIRED GIRL

Our hired girl, she's 'Lizabuth Ann;
An' she can cook best things to eat!
She ist puts dough in our pie-pan,
An' pours in somepin' 'at's good and sweet,
An' nen she salts it all on top
With cinnamon; an' nen she'll stop
An' stoop an' slide it, ist as slow,
In th' old cook-stove, so's 'twon't slop
An' git all spilled; nen bakes it, so
It's custard pie, first thing you know!
An' nen she'll say:
"Clear out o' my way!
They's time fer work, an' time fer play!
Take yer dough, an' run, Child; run!
Er I cain't git no cookin' done!"

When our hired girl 'tends like she's mad,
An' says folks got to walk the chalk
When she's around, er wisht they had,
I play out on our porch an' talk
To th' Raggedy Man 'at mows our lawn;
An' he says "Whew!" an' nen leans on
His old crook-scythe, and blinks his eyes
An' sniffs all around an' says, "I swawn!
Ef my old nose don't tell me lies,
It 'pears like I smell custard-pies!"
An' nen he'll say,
"'Clear out' o' my way!
They's time fer work an' time fer play!
Take yer dough, an' run, Child; run!
Er she cain't git no cookin' done!'"

Wunst our hired girl, one time when she
Got the supper, an' we all et,
An' it was night, an' Ma an' me
An' Pa went wher' the "Social" met,
An' nen when we come home, an' see
A light in the kitchen-door, an' we
Heerd a maccordeum, Pa says "Lan'
O'Gracious! who can her beau be?"

An' I marched in, an' 'Lizabuth Ann
Wuz parchin' corn fer the Raggedy Man!
Better say
"Clear out o' the way!
They's time fer work, an' time fer play!
Take the hint, an' run, Child; run!
Er we cain't git no courtin' done!'"

THE BOYS' CANDIDATE

Las' time 'at Uncle Sidney come,
He bringed a watermelon home
An' half the boys in town,
Come taggin' after him. An' he
Says, when we et it, "Gracious me!
'S the boy-house fell down?"

THE PET COON

Noey Bixler ketched him, and fetched him in to me
When he's ist a little teenty-weenty baby-coon
'Bout as big as little pups, an' tied him to a tree;
An' Pa gived Noey fifty cents, when he come home at noon.
Nen he buyed a chain fer him, an' little collar, too,
An' sawed a hole in a' old tub an' turnt it upside-down;
An' little feller'd stay in there and won't come out fer you
'Tendin' like he's kindo' skeered o' boys 'at lives in town.

Now he aint afeard a bit! he's ist so fat an' tame,
We on'y chain him up at night, to save the little chicks.
Holler "Greedy! Greedy!" to him, an' he knows his name,
An' here he'll come a-waddle-un, up fer any tricks!
He'll climb up my leg, he will, an' waller in my lap,
An' poke his little black paws 'way in my pockets where
They's beechnuts, er chinkypins, er any little scrap
Of anything, 'at's good to eat an' he don't care!

An' he's as spunky as you please, an' don't like dogs at all.
Billy Miller's black-an'-tan tackled him one day,
An' "Greedy" he ist kindo' doubled all up like a ball,
An' Billy's dog he gived a yelp er two an' runned away!
An' nen when Billy fighted me, an' hit me with a bone,
An' Ma she purt'nigh ketched him as he dodged an' skooted thro'
The fence, she says, "You better let my little boy alone,
Er 'Greedy,' next he whips yer dog, shall whip you, too!"

THE OLD HAY-MOW

The Old Hay-mow's the place to play
Fer boys, when it's a rainy day!
I good-'eal ruther be up there
Than down in town, er anywhere!

When I play in our stable-loft,
The good old hay's so dry an' soft,
An' feels so fine, an' smells so sweet,
I 'most ferget to go an' eat.

An' one time wunst I did ferget
To go 'tel dinner was all et,
An' they had short-cake an' Bud he
Hogged up the piece Ma saved fer me!

Nen I won't let him play no more
In our hay-mow where I keep store
An' got hen-eggs to sell, an' shoo
The cackle-un old hen out, too!

An' nen, when Aunty she was here
A-visitun from Rensselaer,
An' bringed my little cousin, he
Can come up there an' play with me.

But, after while when Bud he bets
'At I can't turn no summersetts,
I let him come up, ef he can
Ac' ha'f-way like a gentleman!

ON THE SUNNY SIDE
Hi and whoop-hooray, boys!
Sing a song of cheer!
Here's a holiday, boys,
Lasting half a year!
Round the world, and half is
Shadow we have tried;
Now we're where the laugh is,
On the sunny side!

Pigeons coo and mutter,
Strutting high aloof
Where the sunbeans flutter
Through the stable roof.
Hear the chickens cheep, boys,
And the hen with pride
Clucking them to sleep, boys,
On the sunny side!

Hear the clacking guinea;
Hear the cattle moo;
Hear the horses whinny,
Looking out at you!
On the hitching-block, boys,
Grandly satisfied,
See the old peacock, boys,
On the sunny side!

Robins in the peach-tree;
Bluebirds in the pear;
Blossoms over each tree
In the orchard there!
All the world's in joy, boys,
Glad and glorified
As a romping boy, boys,
On the sunny side!

Where's a heart as mellow?
Where's a soul as free?
Where is any fellow
We would rather be?
Just ourselves or none, boys,
World around and wide,
Laughing in the sun, boys,
On the sunny side!

A SUDDEN SHOWER
Barefooted boys scud up the street
Or skurry under sheltering sheds;
And schoolgirl faces, pale and sweet,
Gleam from the shawls about their heads.

Doors bang; and mother-voices call
From alien homes; and rusty gates
Are slammed; and high above it all,
The thunder grim reverberates.

And then, abrupt, the rain! the rain!
The earth lies gasping; and the eyes
Behind the streaming window-pane
Smile at the trouble of the skies.

The highway smokes; sharp echoes ring;
The cattle bawl and cowbells clank;
And into town comes galloping
The farmer's horse, with streaming flank.

The swallow dips beneath the eaves,

And flirts his plumes and folds his wings;
And under the catawba leaves
The caterpillar curls and clings.

The bumble-bee is pelted down
The wet stem of the hollyhock;
And sullenly, in spattered brown,
The cricket leaps the garden walk.

Within, the baby claps his hands
And crows with rapture strange and vague;
Without, beneath the rosebush stands
A dripping rooster on one leg.

GRANDFATHER SQUEERS

"My grandfather Squeers," said The Raggedy Man,
As he solemnly lighted his pipe and began

"The most indestructible man, for his years,
And the grandest on earth, was my grandfather Squeers!

"He said, when he rounded his three-score-and-ten,
'I've the hang of it now and can do it again!'

"He had frozen his heels so repeatedly, he
Could tell by them just what the weather would be;

"And would laugh and declare, 'while the Almanac would
Most falsely prognosticate, he never could!'

"Such a hale constitution had grandfather Squeers
That, 'though he'd used 'navy' for sixty odd years,

"He still chewed a dime's-worth six days of the week,
While the seventh he passed with a chew in each cheek:

"Then my grandfather Squeers had a singular knack
Of sitting around on the small of his back,

"With his legs like a letter Y stretched o'er the grate
Wherein 'twas his custom to ex-pec-tor-ate.

"He was fond of tobacco in manifold ways,
And would sit on the door-step, of sunshiny days,

"And smoke leaf-tobacco he'd raised strictly for
The pipe he'd used all through The Mexican War."

And The Raggedy Man said, refilling the bowl

Of his own pipe and leisurely picking a coal

From the stove with his finger and thumb, "You can see
What a tee-nacious habit he's fastened on me!

"And my grandfather Squeers took a special delight
In pruning his corns every Saturday night

"With a horn-handled razor, whose edge he excused
By saying 'twas one that his grandfather used;

"And, though deeply etched in the haft of the same
Was the ever-euphonious Wostenholm's name,

"'Twas my grandfather's custom to boast of the blade
As 'A Seth Thomas razor the best ever made!'

"No Old Settlers' Meeting, or Pioneers' Fair,
Was complete without grandfather Squeers in the chair

"To lead off the programme by telling folks how
'He used to shoot deer where the Court-House stands now'

"How 'he felt, of a truth, to live over the past,
When the country was wild and unbroken and vast,

"'That the little log cabin was just plenty fine
For himself, his companion, and fambly of nine!

"'When they didn't have even a pump, or a tin,
But drunk surface-water, year out and year in,

"'From the old-fashioned gourd that was sweeter, by odds,
Than the goblets of gold at the lips of the gods!'"

Then The Raggedy Man paused to plaintively say
It was clockin' along to'rds the close of the day

And he'd ought to get back to his work on the lawn,
Then dreamily blubbered his pipe and went on:

"His teeth were imperfect, my grandfather owned
That he couldn't eat oysters unless they were 'boned';

"And his eyes were so weak, and so feeble of sight,
He couldn't sleep with them unless, every night,

"He put on his spectacles all he possessed,
Three pairs with his goggles on top of the rest.

"And my grandfather always, retiring at night,

Blew down the lamp-chimney to put out the light;

"Then he'd curl up on edge like a shaving, in bed,
And puff and smoke pipes in his sleep, it is said:

"And would snore oftentimes as the legends relate,
Till his folks were wrought up to a terrible state,

"Then he'd snort, and rear up, and roll over; and there,
In the subsequent hush they could hear him chew air.

"And so glaringly bald was the top of his head
That many's the time he has musingly said,

"As his eyes journeyed o'er its reflex in the glass,
'I must set out a few signs of Keep Off the Grass!'

"So remarkably deaf was my grandfather Squeers
That he had to wear lightning-rods over his ears

"To even hear thunder and oftentimes then
He was forced to request it to thunder again."

THE PIXY PEOPLE
It was just a very
Merry fairy dream!
All the woods were airy
With the gloom and gleam;
Crickets in the clover
Clattered clear and strong,
And the bees droned over
Their old honey-song.

In the mossy passes,
Saucy grasshoppers
Leapt about the grasses
And the thistle-burs;
And the whispered chuckle
Of the katydid
Shook the honeysuckle
Blossoms where he hid.

Through the breezy mazes
Of the lazy June,
Drowsy with the hazes
Of the dreamy noon,
Little Pixy people
Winged above the walk,
Pouring from the steeple

Of a mullein-stalk.

One a gallant fellow
Evidently King,
Wore a plume of yellow
In a jewelled ring
On a pansy bonnet,
Gold and white and blue,
With the dew still on it,
And the fragrance, too.

One a dainty lady,
Evidently Queen,
Wore a gown of shady
Moonshine and green,
With a lace of gleaming
Starlight that sent
All the dewdrops dreaming
Everywhere she went.

One wore a waistcoat
Of roseleaves, out and in,
And one wore a faced-coat
Of tiger-lily-skin;
And one wore a neat coat
Of palest galingale;
And one a tiny street-coat,
And one a swallow-tail.

And Ho! sang the King of them,
And Hey! sang the Queen;
And round and round the ring of them
Went dancing o'er the green;
And Hey! sang the Queen of them,
And Ho! sang the King
And all that I had seen of them
Wasn't anything!

It was just a very
Merry fairy dream!
All the woods were airy
With the gloom and gleam;
Crickets in the clover
Clattered clear and strong,
And the bees droned over
Their old honey-song!

A LIFE-LESSON
There! little girl; don't cry!

They have broken your doll, I know;
And your tea-set blue,
And your play-house, too,
Are things of the long ago;
But childish troubles will soon pass by.
There! little girl; don't cry!

There! little girl; don't cry!
They have broken your slate, I know;
And the glad, wild ways
Of your school-girl days
Are things of the long ago;
But life and love will soon come by.
There! little girl; don't cry!

There! little girl; don't cry!
They have broken your heart, I know;
And the rainbow gleams
Of your youthful dreams
Are things of the long ago;
But Heaven holds all for which you sigh.
There! little girl; don't cry!

A HOME-MADE FAIRY-TALE

Bud, come here to your Uncle a spell,
And I'll tell you something you mustn't tell
For it's a secret and shore-nuff true,
And maybe I oughtn't to tell it to you!
But out in the garden, under the shade
Of the apple-trees where we romped and played
Till the moon was up, and you thought I'd gone
Fast asleep. That was all put on!
For I was a-watchin' something queer
Goin' on there in the grass, my dear!
'Way down deep in it, there I see
A little dude-Fairy who winked at me,
And snapped his fingers, and laughed as low
And fine as the whine of a mus-kee-to!
I kept still, watchin' him closer and
I noticed a little guitar in his hand,
Which he leant 'ginst a little dead bee and laid
His cigarette down on a clean grass-blade;
And then climbed up on the shell of a snail
Carefully dusting his swallowtail
And pulling up, by a waxed web-thread,
This little guitar, you remember, I said!
And there he trinkled and trilled a tune
"My Love, so Fair, Tans in the Moon!"
Till presently, out of the clover-top

He seemed to be singing to, came k'pop!
The purtiest, daintiest Fairy face
In all this world, or any place!
Then the little ser'nader waved his hand,
As much as to say, "We'll excuse you!" and
I heard, as I squinted my eyelids to,
A kiss like the drip of a drop of dew!

THE BEAR STORY - THAT ALEX "IST MAKED UP HIS-OWN-SE'F"
W'y, wunst they wuz a Little Boy went out
In the woods to shoot a Bear. So, he went out
'Way in the grea'-big woods, he did. An' he
Wuz goin' along an' goin' along, you know,
An' purty soon he heerd somepin' go "Wooh!"
Ist thataway "Woo-ooh!" An' he wuz skeered,
He wuz. An' so he runned an' clumbed a tree
A grea'-big tree, he did, a sicka-more tree.
An' nen he heerd it ag'in: an' he looked round,
An' 't'uz a Bear! a grea'-big shore-nuff Bear!
No: 't'uz two Bears, it wuz two grea'-big Bears
One of 'em wuz ist one's a grea'-big Bear.
But they ist boff went "Wooh!" An' here they come
To climb the tree an' git the Little Boy
An' eat him up!

An' nen the Little Boy
He 'uz skeered worse'n ever! An' here come
The grea'-big Bear a-climbin' th' tree to git
The Little Boy an' eat him up Oh, no!
It 'uzn't the Big Bear 'at clumb the tree
It 'uz the Little Bear. So here he come
Climbin' the tree an' climbin' the tree! Nen when
He git wite clos't to the Little Boy, w'y nen
The Little Boy he ist pulled up his gun
An' shot the Bear, he did, an' killed him dead!
An' nen the Bear he falled clean on down out
The tree away clean to the ground, he did
Spling-splung! he falled plum down, an' killed him, too!
An' lit wite side o' where the Big Bear's at.

An' nen the Big Bear's awful mad, you bet!
'Cause, 'cause the Little Boy he shot his gun
An' killed the Little Bear. 'Cause the Big Bear
He, he 'uz the Little Bear's Papa. An' so here
He come to climb the big old tree an' git
The Little Boy an' eat him up! An' when
The Little Boy he saw the grea'-big Bear
A-comin', he uz badder skeered, he wuz,
Than any time! An' so he think he'll climb

Up higher 'way up higher in the tree
Than the old Bear kin climb, you know. But he
He can't climb higher 'an old Bears kin climb,
'Cause Bears kin climb up higher in the trees
Than any little Boys in all the Wo-r-r-ld!

An' so here come the grea'-big-Bear, he did,
A-climbin' up an' up the tree, to git
The Little Boy an' eat him up! An' so
The Little Boy he clumbed on higher, an' higher,
An' higher up the tree an' higher, an' higher
An' higher'n iss-here house is! An' here come
Th' old Bear clos'ter to him all the time!
An' nen, first thing you know, when th' old Big Bear
Wuz wite clos't to him, nen the Little Boy
Ist jabbed his gun wite in the old Bear's mouf
An' shot an' killed him dead! No; I fergot,
He didn't shoot the grea'-big Bear at all
'Cause they 'uz no load in the gun, you know
'Cause when he shot the Little Bear, w'y, nen
No load 'uz anymore nen in the gun!

But th' Little Boy clumbed higher up, he did
He clumbed lots higher an' on up higher, an' higher
An' higher tel he ist can't climb no higher,
'Cause nen the limbs 'uz all so little, 'way
Up in the teeny-weeny tip-top of
The tree, they'd break down wiv him ef he don't
Be keerful! So he stop an' think: An' nen
He look around - An' here come th' old Bear!

An' so the Little Boy make up his mind
He's got to ist git out o' there some way!
'Cause here come the old Bear! so clos't, his bref's
Purt 'nigh so's he kin feel how hot it is
Ag'inst his bare feet ist like old "Ring's" bref
When he's ben out a-huntin' an's all tired.
So when th' old Bear's so clos't the Little Boy
Ist gives a grea'-big jump fer 'nother tree
No! no he don't do that! I tell you what
The Little Boy does: W'y, nen, w'y, he - Oh, yes
The Little Boy he finds a hole up there
'At's in the tree an' climbs in there an' hides
An' nen th' old Bear can't find the Little Boy
At all! But, purty soon th' old Bear finds
The Little Boy's gun 'at's up there 'cause the gun
It's too tall to tooked wiv him in the hole.
So, when the old Bear fin' the gun, he knows
The Little Boy's ist hid 'round somers there,
An' th' old Bear 'gins to snuff an' sniff around,
An' sniff an' snuff around so's he kin find

Out where the Little Boy's hid at. An' nen, nen
Oh, yes! W'y, purty soon the old Bear climbs
'Way out on a big limb a grea'-long limb,
An' nen the Little Boy climbs out the hole
An' takes his ax an' chops the limb off!... Nen
The old Bear falls k-splunge! clean to the ground
An' bust an' kill hisse'f plum dead, he did!

An' nen the Little Boy he git his gun
An' 'menced a-climbin' down the tree ag'in
No! no, he didn't git his gun 'cause when
The Bear falled, nen the gun falled, too. An' broked
It all to pieces, too! An' nicest gun!
His Pa ist buyed it! An' the Little Boy
Ist cried, he did; an' went on climbin' down
The tree, an' climbin' down, an' climbin' down!
An'-sir! when he 'uz purt'-nigh down, w'y, nen
The old Bear he jumped up ag'in, an' he
Ain't dead at all, ist 'tendin' thataway,
So he kin git the Little Boy an' eat
Him up! But the Little Boy he 'uz too smart
To climb clean down the tree. An' the old Bear
He can't climb up the tree no more, 'cause when
He fell, he broke one of his, he broke all
His legs! an' nen he couldn't climb! But he
Ist won't go'way an' let the Little Boy
Come down out of the tree. An' the old Bear
Ist growls 'round there, he does ist growls an' goes
"Wooh! woo-ooh!" all the time! An' Little Boy
He haf to stay up in the tree all night
An' 'thout no supper neether! On'y they
Wuz apples on the tree! An' Little Boy
Et apples ist all night an' cried, an' cried!
Nen when 'tuz morning th' old Bear went "Wooh!"
Ag'in, an' try to climb up in the tree
An' git the Little Boy. But he can't
Climb t'save his soul, he can't! An' oh! he's mad!
He ist tear up the ground! an' go "Woo-ooh!"
An' Oh, yes! purty soon, when morning's come
All light so's you kin see, you know, w'y, nen
The old Bear finds the Little Boy's gun, you know,
'At's on the ground. (An' it ain't broke at all
I ist said that!) An' so the old Bear think
He'll take the gun an' shoot the Little Boy:
But Bears they don't know much 'bout shootin' guns;
So when he go to shoot the Little Boy,
The old Bear got the other end the gun
Ag'in' his shoulder, 'stid o' th' other end
So when he try to shoot the Little Boy,
It shot the Bear, it did an' killed him dead!
An' nen the Little Boy clumb down the tree

An' chopped his old woolly head off: Yes, an' killed
The other Bear ag'in, he did an' killed
All boff the bears, he did an' tuk 'em home
An' cooked 'em, too, an' et 'em!
An' that's all.

ENVOY
Many pleasures of youth have been buoyantly sung
And, borne on the winds of delight, may they beat
With their palpitant wings at the hearts of the Young,
And in bosoms of Age find as warm a retreat!
Yet sweetest of all of the musical throng,
Though least of the numbers that upward aspire,
Is the one rising now into wavering song,
As I sit in the silence and gaze in the fire.

'Tis a Winter long dead that beleaguers my door
And muffles his steps in the snows of the past:
And I see, in the embers I'm dreaming before,
Lost faces of love as they looked on me last:
The round, laughing eyes of the desk-mate of old
Gleam out for a moment with truant desire
Then fade and are lost in a City of Gold,
As I sit in the silence and gaze in the fire.

And then comes the face, peering back in my own,
Of a shy little girl, with her lids drooping low,
As she faltering tells, in a far-away tone,
The ghost of a story of long, long ago.
Then her dewy blue eyes they are lifted again;
But I see their glad light slowly fail and expire,
As I reach and cry to her in vain, all in vain!
As I sit in the silence and gaze in the fire.

Then the face of a Mother looks back, through the mist
Of tears that are welling; and, lucent with light,
I see the dear smile of the lips I have kissed
As she knelt by my cradle at morning and night;
And my arms are outheld, with a yearning too wild
For any but God in His love to inspire,
As she pleads at the foot of His throne for her child,
As I sit in the silence and gaze in the fire.

O pathos of rapture! O glorious pain!
My heart is a blossom of joy over-run
With a shower of tears, as a lily with rain
That weeps in the shadow and laughs in the sun.
The blight of the frost may descend on the tree,
And the leaf and the flower may fall and expire,
But ever and ever love blossoms for me,
As I sit in the silence and gaze in the fire.

Farm-Rhymes

TO THE GOOD OLD-FASHIONED PEOPLE

The deadnin' and the thicket's jes' a b'ilin' full o' June,
From the rattle o' the cricket, to the yaller-hammer's tune;
And the catbird in the bottom and the sap-suck on the snag,
Seems's ef they cain't od-rot-'em! jes' do nothin' else but brag!

There' music in the twitter o' the bluebird and the jay,
And that sassy little critter jes' a-peckin' all the day;
There' music in the "flicker," and there' music in the thrush,
And there' music in the snicker o' the chipmunk in the brush!

There' music all around me! And I go back in a dream
Sweeter yit than ever found me fast asleep: And, in the stream
That used to split the medder wher' the dandylions growed,
I stand knee-deep, and redder than the sunset down the road.

THE ORCHARD LANDS OF LONG AGO
The orchard lands of Long Ago!
O drowsy winds, awake, and blow
The snowy blossoms back to me,
And all the buds that used to be!
Blow back along the grassy ways
Of truant feet, and lift the haze
Of happy summer from the trees
That trail their tresses in the seas
Of grain that float and overflow
The orchard lands of Long Ago!

Blow back the melody that slips
In lazy laughter from the lips
That marvel much if any kiss
Is sweeter than the apple's is.
Blow back the twitter of the birds
The lisp, the titter, and the words
Of merriment that found the shine
Of summer-time a glorious wine
That drenched the leaves that loved it so,
In orchard lands of Long Ago!

O memory! alight and sing
Where rosy-bellied pippins cling,
And golden russets glint and gleam,

As, in the old Arabian dream,
The fruits of that enchanted tree
The glad Aladdin robbed for me!
And, drowsy winds, awake and fan
My blood as when it overran
A heart ripe as the apples grow
In orchard lands of Long Ago!

WHEN THE FROST IS ON THE PUNKIN

When the frost is on the punkin and the fodder's in the shock,
And you hear the kyouck and gobble of the struttin' turkey-cock,
And the clackin' of the guineys, and the cluckin' of the hens,
And the rooster's hallylooyer as he tiptoes on the fence;
O, it's then's the times a feller is a-feelin' at his best,
With the risin' sun to greet him from a night of peaceful rest,
As he leaves the house, bare-headed, and goes out to feed the stock,
When the frost is on the punkin and the fodder's in the shock.

They's something kindo' harty-like about the atmusfere
When the heat of summer's over and the coolin' fall is here
Of course we miss the flowers, and the blossums on the trees,
And the mumble of the hummin'-birds and buzzin' of the bees;
But the air's so appetizin'; and the landscape through the haze
Of a crisp and sunny morning of the airly autumn days
Is a pictur' that no painter has the colorin' to mock
When the frost is on the punkin and the fodder's in the shock.

The husky, rusty russel of the tossels of the corn,
And the raspin' of the tangled leaves, as golden as the morn;
The stubble in the furries kindo' lonesome-like, but still
A-preachin' sermuns to us of the barns they growed to fill;
The strawstack in the medder, and the reaper in the shed;
The hosses in theyr stalls below the clover overhead!
O, it sets my hart a-clickin' like the tickin' of a clock,
When the frost is on the punkin and the fodder's in the shock!

Then your apples all is getherd, and the ones a feller keeps
Is poured around the cellar-floor in red and yeller heaps;
And your cider-makin's over, and your wimmern-folks is through
With their mince and apple-butter, and theyr souse and saussage, too!...
I don't know how to tell it but ef sich a thing could be
As the Angels wantin' boardin', and they'd call around on ME
I'd want to 'commodate 'em, all the whole-indurin' flock
When the frost is on the punkin and the fodder's in the shock!

WHEN THE GREEN GITS BACK IN THE TREES

In Spring, when the green gits back in the trees,

And the sun comes out and STAYS,
And yer boots pulls on with a good tight squeeze,
And you think of yer bare-foot days;
When you ORT to work and you want to NOT,
And you and yer wife agrees
It's time to spade up the garden-lot,
When the green gits back in the trees
Well! work is the least o' MY idees
When the green, you know, gits back in the trees!

When the green gits back in the trees, and bees
Is a-buzzin' aroun' ag'in
In that kind of a lazy go-as-you-please
Old gait they bum roun' in;
When the groun's all bald whare the hay-rick stood,
And the crick's riz, and the breeze
Coaxes the bloom in the old dogwood,
And the green gits back in the trees,
I like, as I say, in sich scenes as these,
The time when the green gits back in the trees!

When the whole tail-feathers o' Wintertime
Is all pulled out and gone!
And the sap it thaws and begins to climb,
And the swet it starts out on
A feller's forred, a-gittin' down
At the old spring on his knees
I kindo' like jest a-loaferin' roun'
When the green gits back in the trees
Jest a-potterin' roun' as I durn please
When the green, you know, gits back in the trees!

WET-WEATHER TALK
It hain't no use to grumble and complane;
It's jest as cheap and easy to rejoice.
When God sorts out the weather and sends rain,
W'y, rain's my choice.

Men ginerly, to all intents
Although they're apt to grumble some
Puts most theyr trust in Providence,
And takes things as they come
That is, the commonality
Of men that's lived as long as me
Has watched the world enugh to learn
They're not the boss of this concern.

With SOME, of course, it's different
I've saw YOUNG men that knowed it all,

And didn't like the way things went
On this terrestchul ball;
But all the same, the rain, some way,
Rained jest as hard on picnic day;
Er, when they railly WANTED it,
It mayby wouldn't rain a bit!

In this existunce, dry and wet
Will overtake the best of men
Some little skift o' clouds'll shet
The sun off now and then.
And mayby, whilse you're wundern who
You've fool-like lent your umbrell' to,
And WANT it, out'll pop the sun,
And you'll be glad you hain't got none!

It aggervates the farmers, too
They's too much wet, er too much sun,
Er work, er waitin' round to do
Before the plowin' 's done:
And mayby, like as not, the wheat,
Jest as it's lookin' hard to beat,
Will ketch the storm and jest about
The time the corn's a-jintin' out.

These-here CY-CLONES a-foolin' round
And back'ard crops! and wind and rain!
And yit the corn that's wallerd down
May elbow up again!
They hain't no sense, as I can see,
Fer mortuls, sich as us, to be
A-faultin' Natchur's wise intents,
And lockin' horns with Providence!

It hain't no use to grumble and complane;
It's jest as cheap and easy to rejoice.
When God sorts out the weather and sends rain,
W'y, rain's my choice.

THE BROOK-SONG
Little brook! Little brook!
You have such a happy look
Such a very merry manner, as you swerve and curve and crook
And your ripples, one and one,
Reach each other's hands and run
Like laughing little children in the sun!

Little brook, sing to me:
Sing about a bumblebee

That tumbled from a lily-bell and grumbled mumblingly,
Because he wet the film
Of his wings, and had to swim,
While the water-bugs raced round and laughed at him!

Little brook-sing a song
Of a leaf that sailed along
Down the golden-braided centre of your current swift and strong,
And a dragon-fly that lit
On the tilting rim of it,
And rode away and wasn't scared a bit.

And sing, how oft in glee
Came a truant boy like me,
Who loved to lean and listen to your lilting melody,
Till the gurgle and refrain
Of your music in his brain
Wrought a happiness as keen to him as pain.

Little brook-laugh and leap!
Do not let the dreamer weep:
Sing him all the songs of summer till he sink in softest sleep;
And then sing soft and low
Through his dreams of long ago
Sing back to him the rest he used to know!

THOUGHTS FER THE DISCURAGED FARMER
The summer winds is sniffin' round the bloomin' locus' trees;
And the clover in the pastur is a big day fer the bees,
And they been a-swiggin' honey, above board and on the sly,
Tel they stutter in theyr buzzin' and stagger as they fly.
The flicker on the fence-rail 'pears to jest spit on his wings
And roll up his feathers, by the sassy way he sings;
And the hoss-fly is a-whettin'-up his forelegs fer biz,
And the off-mare is a-switchin' all of her tale they is.

You can hear the blackbirds jawin' as they foller up the plow
Oh, theyr bound to git theyr brekfast, and theyr not a-carin' how;
So they quarrel in the furries, and they quarrel on the wing
But theyr peaceabler in pot-pies than any other thing:
And it's when I git my shotgun drawed up in stiddy rest,
She's as full of tribbelation as a yeller-jacket's nest;
And a few shots before dinner, when the sun's a-shinin' right,
Seems to kindo'-sorto' sharpen up a feller's appetite!

They's been a heap o' rain, but the sun's out to-day,
And the clouds of the wet spell is all cleared away,
And the woods is all the greener, and the grass is greener still;
It may rain again to-morry, but I don't think it will.

Some says the crops is ruined, and the corn's drownded out,
And propha-sy the wheat will be a failure, without doubt;
But the kind Providence that has never failed us yet,
Will be on hands onc't more at the 'leventh hour, I bet!

Does the medder-lark complane, as he swims high and dry
Through the waves of the wind and the blue of the sky?
Does the quail set up and whissel in a disappinted way,
Er hang his head in silunce, and sorrow all the day?
Is the chipmuck's health a-failin'? Does he walk, er does he run?
Don't the buzzards ooze around up thare just like they've allus done?
Is they anything the matter with the rooster's lungs er voice?
Ort a mortul be complainin' when dumb animals rejoice?

Then let us, one and all, be contentud with our lot;
The June is here this morning, and the sun is shining hot.
Oh! let us fill our harts up with the glory of the day,
And banish ev'ry doubt and care and sorrow fur away!
Whatever be our station, with Providence fer guide,
Sich fine circumstances ort to make us satisfied;
Fer the world is full of roses, and the roses full of dew,
And the dew is full of heavenly love that drips fer me and you.

"MYLO JONES'S WIFE"
"Mylo Jones's wife" was all
I heerd, mighty near, last Fall
Visitun relations down
T'other side of Morgantown!
Mylo Jones's wife she does
This and that, and "those" and "thus"!
Can't 'bide babies in her sight
Ner no childern, day and night,
Whoopin' round the premises
NER NO NOTHIN' ELSE, I guess!

Mylo Jones's wife she 'lows
She's the boss of her own house!
Mylo consequences is
Stays whare things seem SOME like HIS,
Uses, mostly, with the stock
Coaxin' "Old Kate" not to balk,
Ner kick hoss-flies' branes out, ner
Act, I s'pose, so much like HER!
Yit the wimmern-folks tells you
She's PERFECTION. Yes they do!

Mylo's wife she says she's found
Home hain't home with MEN-FOLKS round
When they's work like HERN to do

Picklin' pears and BUTCHERN, too,
And a-rendern lard, and then
Cookin' fer a pack of men
To come trackin' up the flore
SHE'S scrubbed TEL she'll scrub no MORE!
Yit she'd keep things clean ef they
Made her scrub tel Jedgmunt Day!

Mylo Jones's wife she sews
Carpet-rags and patches clothes
Jest year IN and OUT! and yit
Whare's the livin' use of it?
She asts Mylo that. And he
Gits back whare he'd ruther be,
With his team; jest PLOWS and don't
Never sware like some folks won't!
Think ef HE'D CUT LOOSE, I gum!
'D he'p his heavenly chances some!

Mylo's wife don't see no use,
Ner no reason ner excuse
Fer his pore relations to
Hang round like they allus do!
Thare 'bout onc't a year and SHE
She jest GA'NTS 'em, folks tells me,
On spiced pears! Pass Mylo one,
He says "No, he don't chuse none!"
Workin'men like Mylo they
'D ort to have MEAT ev'ry day!

Dad-burn Mylo Jones's wife!
Ruther rake a blame caseknife
'Crost my wizzen than to see
Sich a womern rulin' ME!
Ruther take and turn in and
Raise a fool mule-colt by hand'
MYLO, though od-rot the man!
Jest keeps ca'm like some folks CAN
And 'lows sich as her, I s'pose,
Is MAN'S HE'PMEET' Mercy knows!

HOW JOHN QUIT THE FARM

Nobody on the old farm here but Mother, me and John,
Except, of course, the extry he'p when harvest-time comes on,
And THEN, I want to say to you, we NEEDED he'p about,
As you'd admit, ef you'd a-seen the way the crops turned out!

A better quarter-section ner a richer soil warn't found
Than this-here old-home place o' ourn fer fifty miles around!

The house was small but plenty-big we found it from the day
That John, our only livin' son, packed up and went away.

You see, we tuk sich pride in John, his mother more'n me
That's natchurul; but BOTH of us was proud as proud could be;
Fer the boy, from a little chap, was most oncommon bright,
And seemed in work as well as play to take the same delight.

He allus went a-whistlin' round the place, as glad at heart
As robins up at five o'clock to git an airly start;
And many a time 'fore daylight Mother's waked me up to say
"Jest listen, David! listen! Johnny's beat the birds to-day!"

High-sperited from boyhood, with a most inquirin' turn,
He wanted to learn ever'thing on earth they was to learn:
He'd ast more plaguy questions in a mortal-minute here
Than his grandpap in Paradise could answer in a year!

And READ! w'y, his own mother learnt him how to read and spell;
And "The Childern of the Abbey" w'y, he knowed that book as well
At fifteen as his parents! and "The Pilgrim's Progress," too
Jest knuckled down, the shaver did, and read 'em through and through.

At eighteen, Mother 'lowed the boy must have a better chance-
That we ort to educate him, under any circumstance;
And John he j'ined his mother, and they ding-donged and kep' on,
Tel I sent him off to school in town, half glad that he was gone.

But I missed him w'y, of course I did! The Fall and Winter through
I never built the kitchen-fire, er split a stick in two,
Er fed the stock, er butchered, er swung up a gambrel-pin,
But what I thought o' John, and wished that he was home ag'in.

He'd come, sometimes on Sund'ys most, and stay the Sund'y out;
And on Thanksgivin'-Day he 'peared to like to be about:
But a change was workin' on him, he was stiller than before,
And didn't joke, ner laugh, ner sing and whistle any more.

And his talk was all so proper; and I noticed, with a sigh,
He was tryin' to raise side-whiskers, and had on a striped tie,
And a standin'-collar, ironed up as stiff and slick as bone;
And a breast-pin, and a watch and chain and plug-hat of his own.

But when Spring-weather opened out, and John was to come home
And he'p me through the season, I was glad to see him come,
But my happiness, that evening, with the settin' sun went down,
When he bragged of "a position" that was offered him in town.

"But," says I, "you'll not accept it?" "W'y, of course I will," says he.
"This drudgin' on a farm," he says, "is not the life fer me;
I've set my stakes up higher," he continued, light and gay,

"And town's the place fer ME, and I'm a-goin' right away!"

And go he did! his mother clingin' to him at the gate,
A-pleadin' and a-cryin'; but it hadn't any weight.
I was tranquiller, and told her 'twarn't no use to worry so,
And onclasped her arms from round his neck round mine and let him go!

I felt a little bitter feelin' foolin' round about
The aidges of my conscience; but I didn't let it out;
I simply retch out, trimbly-like, and tuk the boy's hand,
And though I didn't say a word, I knowed he'd understand.

And well! sence then the old home here was mighty lonesome, shore!
With me a-workin' in the field, and Mother at the door,
Her face ferever to'rds the town, and fadin' more and more
Her only son nine miles away, a-clerkin' in a store!

The weeks and months dragged by us; and sometimes the boy would write
A letter to his mother, sayin' that his work was light,
And not to feel oneasy about his health a bit
Though his business was confinin', he was gittin' used to it.

And sometimes he would write and ast how I was gittin' on,
And ef I had to pay out much fer he'p sence he was gone;
And how the hogs was doin', and the balance of the stock,
And talk on fer a page er two jest like he used to talk.

And he wrote, along 'fore harvest, that he guessed he would git home,
Fer business would, of course, be dull in town. But DIDN'T come:
We got a postal later, sayin' when they had no trade
They filled the time "invoicin' goods," and that was why he stayed.

And then he quit a-writin' altogether: Not a word
Exceptin' what the neighbors brung who'd been to town and heard
What store John was clerkin' in, and went round to inquire
If they could buy their goods there less and sell their produce higher.

And so the Summer faded out, and Autumn wore away,
And a keener Winter never fetched around Thanksgivin' Day!
The night before that day of thanks I'll never quite fergit,
The wind a-howlin' round the house-it makes me creepy yit!

And there set me and Mother, me a-twistin' at the prongs
Of a green scrub-ellum forestick with a vicious pair of tongs,
And Mother sayin', "DAVID! DAVID!" in a' undertone,
As though she thought that I was thinkin' bad-words unbeknown.

"I've dressed the turkey, David, fer to-morrow," Mother said,
A-tryin' to wedge some pleasant subject in my stubborn head,
"And the mince-meat I'm a-mixin' is perfection mighty nigh;
And the pound-cake is delicious-rich, " "Who'll eat 'em?" I, says I.

"The cramberries is drippin'-sweet," says Mother, runnin' on,
P'tendin' not to hear me; "and somehow I thought of John
All the time they was a-jellin', fer you know they allus was
His favorITE, he likes 'em so!" Says I "Well, s'pose he does?"

"Oh, nothin' much!" says Mother, with a quiet sort o' smile
"This gentleman behind my cheer may tell you after while!"
And as I turnt and looked around, some one riz up and leant
And putt his arms round Mother's neck, and laughed in low content.

"It's ME," he says, "your fool-boy John, come back to shake your hand;
Set down with you, and talk with you, and make you understand
How dearer yit than all the world is this old home that we
Will spend Thanksgivin' in fer life, jest Mother, you and me!"

Nobody on the old farm here but Mother, me and John,
Except, of course, the extry he'p when harvest-time comes on;
And then, I want to say to you, we NEED sich he'p about,
As you'd admit, ef you could see the way the crops turn out!

A CANARY AT THE FARM
Folks has be'n to town, and Sahry
Fetched 'er home a pet canary,
And of all the blame', contrary,
Aggervatin' things alive!
I love music, that's I love it
When it's free, and plenty of it;
But I kindo' git above it,
At a dollar-eighty-five!

Reason's plain as I'm a sayin',
Jes' the idy, now, o' layin'
Out yer money, and a-payin'
Fer a wilder-cage and bird,
When the medder-larks is wingin'
Round you, and the woods is ringin'
With the beautifullest singin'
That a mortal ever heard!

Sahry's sot, tho'. So I tell her
He's a purty little feller,
With his wings o' creamy-yeller,
And his eyes keen as a cat;
And the twitter o' the critter
Tears to absolutely glitter!
Guess I'll haf to go and git her
A high-priceter cage 'n that!

WHERE THE CHILDREN USED TO PLAY

The old farm-home is Mother's yet and mine,
And filled it is with plenty and to spare,
But we are lonely here in life's decline,
Though fortune smiles around us everywhere:
We look across the gold
Of the harvests, as of old
The corn, the fragrant clover, and the hay
But most we turn our gaze,
As with eyes of other days,
To the orchard where the children used to play.

O from our life's full measure
And rich hoard of worldly treasure
We often turn our weary eyes away,
And hand in hand we wander
Down the old path winding yonder
To the orchard where the children used to play

Our sloping pasture-lands are filled with herds;
The barn and granary-bins are bulging o'er:
The grove's a paradise of singing birds-
The woodland brook leaps laughing by the door
Yet lonely, lonely still,
Let us prosper as we will,
Our old hearts seem so empty everyway
We can only through a mist
See the faces we have kissed
In the orchard where the children used to play.

O from our life's full measure
And rich hoard of worldly treasure
We often turn our weary eyes away,
And hand in hand we wander
Down the old path winding yonder
To the orchard where the children used to play.

GRIGGSBY'S STATION

Pap's got his pattent-right, and rich as all creation;
But where's the peace and comfort that we all had before?
Le's go a-visitin' back to Griggsby's Station
Back where we ust to be so happy and so pore!

The likes of us a-livin' here! It's jest a mortal pity
To see us in this great big house, with cyarpets on the stairs,
And the pump right in the kitchen! And the city! city! city!
And nothin' but the city all around us ever'wheres!

Climb clean above the roof and look from the steeple,
And never see a robin, nor a beech or ellum tree!
And right here in ear-shot of at least a thousan' people,
And none that neighbors with us or we want to go and see!

Le's go a-visitin' back to Griggsby's Station
Back where the latch-string's a-hangin' from the door,
And ever' neighbor round the place is dear as a relation
Back where we ust to be so happy and so pore!

I want to see the Wiggenses, the whole kit-and-bilin',
A-drivin' up from Shallor Ford to stay the Sunday through;
And I want to see 'em hitchin' at their son-in-law's and pilin'
Out there at 'Lizy Ellen's like they ust to do!

I want to see the piece-quilts the Jones girls is makin';
And I want to pester Laury 'bout their freckled hired hand,
And joke her 'bout the widower she come purt' nigh a-takin',
Till her Pap got his pension 'lowed in time to save his land.

Le's go a-visitin' back to Griggsby's Station
Back where they's nothin' aggervatin' any more,
Shet away safe in the woods around the old location
Back where we ust to be so happy and so pore!

I want to see Marindy and he'p her with her sewin',
And hear her talk so lovin' of her man that's dead and gone,
And stand up with Emanuel to show me how he's growin',
And smile as I have saw her 'fore she putt her mournin' on.

And I want to see the Samples, on the old lower eighty,
Where John, our oldest boy, he was tuk and buried for
His own sake and Katy's, and I want to cry with Katy
As she reads all his letters over, writ from The War.

What's in all this grand life and high situation,
And nary pink nor hollyhawk a-bloomin' at the door?
Le's go a-visitin' back to Griggsby's Station
Back where we ust to be so happy and so pore!

KNEE-DEEP IN JUNE

I

Tell you what I like the best
'Long about knee-deep in June,
'Bout the time strawberries melts
On the vine, some afternoon
Like to jes' git out and rest,
And not work at nothin' else'

II
Orchard's where I'd ruther be
Needn't fence it in fer me!
Jes' the whole sky overhead,
And the whole airth underneath
Sorto' so's a man kin breathe
Like he ort, and kindo' has
Elbow-room to keerlessly
Sprawl out len'thways on the grass
Where the shadders thick and soft
As the kivvers on the bed
Mother fixes in the loft
Allus, when they's company!

III
Jes' a-sorto' lazin' there
S'lazy, 'at you peek and peer
Through the wavin' leaves above,
Like a feller 'at's in love
And don't know it, ner don't keer!
Ever'thing you hear and see
Got some sort o' interest
Maybe find a bluebird's nest
Tucked up there conveenently
Fer the boy 'at's ap' to be
Up some other apple-tree!
Watch the swallers skootin' past
'Bout as peert as you could ast,
Er the Bob-white raise and whiz
Where some other's whistle is

IV
Ketch a shadder down below,
And look up to find the crow
Er a hawk, away up there,
'Pearantly FROZE in the air!
Hear the old hen squawk, and squat
Over ever' chick she's got,
Suddent-like! and she knows where
That-air hawk is, well as you!
You jes' bet yer life she do!
Eyes a-glitterin' like glass,
Waitin' till he makes a pass!

V
Pee-wees' singin', to express
My opinion, 's second class,
Yit you'll hear 'em more er less;
Sapsucks gittin' down to biz,
Weedin' out the lonesomeness;

Mr. Bluejay, full o' sass,
In them base-ball clothes o' his,
Sportin' round the orchard jes'
Like he owned the premises!
Sun out in the fields kin sizz,
But flat on yer back, I guess,
In the shade's where glory is!
That's jes' what I'd like to do
Stiddy fer a year er two!

VI

Plague! ef they ain't somepin' in
Work 'at kindo' goes ag'in'
My convictions! 'long about
Here in June especially!
Under some old apple-tree,
Jes' a-restin' through and through
I could git along without
Nothin' else at all to do
Only jes' a-wishin' you
Wuz a-gittin' there like me,
And June was eternity!

VII

Lay out there and try to see
Jes' how lazy you kin be!
Tumble round and souse yer head
In the clover-bloom, er pull
Yer straw hat acrost yer eyes
And peek through it at the skies,
Thinkin' of old chums 'at's dead,
Maybe, smilin' back at you
In betwixt the beautiful
Clouds o' gold and white and blue.
Month a man kin railly love
June, you know, I'm talkin' of!

VIII

March ain't never nothin' new!
Aprile's altogether too
Brash fer me! and May I jes'
'Bominate its promises,
Little hints o' sunshine and
Green around the timber-land
A few blossoms, and a few
Chip-birds, and a sprout er two,
Drap asleep, and it turns in
'Fore daylight and SNOWS ag'in!
But when JUNE comes. Clear my th'oat
With wild honey! Rench my hair
In the dew! and hold my coat!

Whoop out loud! and th'ow my hat!
June wants me, and I'm to spare!
Spread them shadders anywhere,
I'll git down and waller there,
And obleeged to you at that!

SEPTEMBER DARK
I
The air falls chill;
The whippoorwill
Pipes lonesomely behind the hill:
The dusk grows dense,
The silence tense;
And lo, the katydids commence.

II
Through shadowy rifts
Of woodland, lifts
The low, slow moon, and upward drifts,
While left and right
The fireflies' light
Swirls eddying in the skirts of Night.

III
O Cloudland, gray
And level, lay
Thy mists across the face of Day!
At foot and head,
Above the dead,
O Dews, weep on uncomforted!

THE CLOVER
Some sings of the lily, and daisy, and rose,
And the pansies and pinks that the Summertime throws
In the green grassy lap of the medder that lays
Blinkin' up at the skyes through the sunshiney days;
But what is the lily and all of the rest
Of the flowers, to a man with a hart in his brest
That was dipped brimmin' full of the honey and dew
Of the sweet clover-blossoms his babyhood knew?
I never set eyes on a clover-field now,
Er fool round a stable, er climb in the mow,
But my childhood comes back jest as clear and as plane
As the smell of the clover I'm sniffin' again;
And I wunder away in a bare-footed dream,
Whare I tangle my toes in the blossoms that gleam
With the dew of the dawn of the morning of love
Ere it wept ore the graves that I'm weepin' above.

And so I love clover it seems like a part
Of the sacerdest sorrows and joys of my hart;
And wharever it blossoms, oh, thare let me bow
And thank the good God as I'm thankin' Him now;
And I pray to Him still fer the stren'th when I die,
To go out in the clover and tell it good-bye,
And lovin'ly nestle my face in its bloom
While my soul slips away on a breth of purfume

OLD OCTOBER
Old October's purt' nigh gone,
And the frosts is comin' on
Little HEAVIER every day
Like our hearts is thataway!
Leaves is changin' overhead
Back from green to gray and red,
Brown and yeller, with their stems
Loosenin' on the oaks and e'ms;
And the balance of the trees
Gittin' balder every breeze
Like the heads we're scratchin' on!
Old October's purt' nigh gone.

I love Old October so,
I can't bear to see her go
Seems to me like losin' some
Old-home relative er chum
'Pears like sorto' settin' by
Some old friend 'at sigh by sigh
Was a-passin' out o' sight
Into everlastin' night!
Hickernuts a feller hears
Rattlin' down is more like tears
Drappin' on the leaves below
I love Old October so!

Can't tell what it is about
Old October knocks me out!
I sleep well enough at night
And the blamedest appetite
Ever mortal man possessed,
Last thing et, it tastes the best!
Warnuts, butternuts, pawpaws,
'Iles and limbers up my jaws
Fer raal service, sich as new
Pork, spareribs, and sausage, too.
Yit, fer all, they's somepin' 'bout
Old October knocks me out!

OLD-FASHIONED ROSES

They ain't no style about 'em,
And they're sorto' pale and faded,
Yit the doorway here, without 'em,
Would be lonesomer, and shaded
With a good 'eal blacker shadder
Than the morning-glories makes,
And the sunshine would look sadder
Fer their good old-fashion' sakes,

I like 'em 'cause they kindo'
Sorto' MAKE a feller like 'em!
And I tell you, when I find a
Bunch out whur the sun kin strike 'em,
It allus sets me thinkin'
O' the ones 'at used to grow
And peek in thro' the chinkin'
O' the cabin, don't you know!

And then I think o' mother,
And how she ust to love 'em
When they wuzn't any other,
'Less she found 'em up above 'em!
And her eyes, afore she shut 'em,
Whispered with a smile and said
We must pick a bunch and putt 'em
In her hand when she wuz dead.

But, as I wuz a-sayin',
They ain't no style about 'em
Very gaudy er displaying
But I wouldn't be without 'em,
'Cause I'm happier in these posies,
And the hollyhawks and sich,
Than the hummin'-bird 'at noses
In the roses of the rich.

A COUNTRY PATHWAY

I come upon it suddenly, alone
A little pathway winding in the weeds
That fringe the roadside; and with dreams my own,
I wander as it leads.

Full wistfully along the slender way,
Through summer tan of freckled shade and shine,
I take the path that leads me as it may

Its every choice is mine.

A chipmunk, or a sudden-whirring quail,
Is startled by my step as on I fare
A garter-snake across the dusty trail
Glances and is not there.

Above the arching jimson-weeds flare twos
And twos of sallow-yellow butterflies,
Like blooms of lorn primroses blowing loose
When autumn winds arise.

The trail dips, dwindles, broadens then, and lifts
Itself astride a cross-road dubiously,
And, from the fennel marge beyond it, drifts
Still onward, beckoning me.

And though it needs must lure me mile on mile
Out of the public highway, still I go,
My thoughts, far in advance in Indian-file,
Allure me even so.

Why, I am as a long-lost boy that went
At dusk to bring the cattle to the bars,
And was not found again, though Heaven lent
His mother all the stars

With which to seek him through that awful night.
O years of nights as vain! Stars never rise
But well might miss their glitter in the light
Of tears in mother-eyes!

So on, with quickened breaths, I follow still
My avant-courier must be obeyed!
Thus am I led, and thus the path, at will,
Invites me to invade

A meadow's precincts, where my daring guide
Clambers the steps of an old-fashioned stile,
And stumbles down again, the other side,
To gambol there awhile

In pranks of hide-and-seek, as on ahead
I see it running, while the clover-stalks
Shake rosy fists at me, as though they said
"You dog our country walks

"And mutilate us with your walking-stick!
We will not suffer tamely what you do,
And warn you at your peril, for we'll sic
Our bumblebees on you!"

But I smile back, in airy nonchalance,
The more determined on my wayward quest,
As some bright memory a moment dawns
A morning in my breast

Sending a thrill that hurries me along
In faulty similes of childish skips,
Enthused with lithe contortions of a song
Performing on my lips.

In wild meanderings o'er pasture wealth
Erratic wanderings through dead'ning-lands,
Where sly old brambles, plucking me by stealth,
Put berries in my hands:

Or the path climbs a bowlder, wades a slough
Or, rollicking through buttercups and flags,
Goes gayly dancing o'er a deep bayou
On old tree-trunks and snags:

Or, at the creek, leads o'er a limpid pool
Upon a bridge the stream itself has made,
With some Spring-freshet for the mighty tool
That its foundation laid.

I pause a moment here to bend and muse,
With dreamy eyes, on my reflection, where
A boat-backed bug drifts on a helpless cruise,
Or wildly oars the air,

As, dimly seen, the pirate of the brook
The pike, whose jaunty hulk denotes his speed
Swings pivoting about, with wary look
Of low and cunning greed.

Till, filled with other thought, I turn again
To where the pathway enters in a realm
Of lordly woodland, under sovereign reign
Of towering oak and elm.

A puritanic quiet here reviles
The almost whispered warble from the hedge.
And takes a locust's rasping voice and files
The silence to an edge.

In such a solitude my sombre way
Strays like a misanthrope within a gloom
Of his own shadows till the perfect day
Bursts into sudden bloom,

And crowns a long, declining stretch of space,
Where King Corn's armies lie with flags unfurled.
And where the valley's dint in Nature's face
Dimples a smiling world.

And lo! through mists that may not be dispelled,
I see an old farm homestead, as in dreams,
Where, like a gem in costly setting held,
The old log cabin gleams.

O darling Pathway! lead me bravely on
Adown your alley-way, and run before
Among the roses crowding up the lawn
And thronging at the door,

And carry up the echo there that shall
Arouse the drowsy dog, that he may bay
The household out to greet the prodigal
That wanders home to-day.

WORTERMELON TIME

Old wortermelon time is a-comin' round again,
And they ain't no man a-livin' any tickleder'n me,
Fer the way I hanker after wortermelons is a sin
Which is the why and wharefore, as you can plainly see.

Oh! it's in the sandy soil wortermelons does the best,
And it's thare they'll lay and waller in the sunshine andthe dew
Tel they wear all the green streaks clean off of theyr breast;
And you bet I ain't a-findin' any fault with them; ain't you?

They ain't no better thing in the vegetable line;
And they don't need much 'tendin', as ev'ry farmer knows;
And when theyr ripe and ready fer to pluck from the vine,
I want to say to you theyr the best fruit that grows.

It's some likes the yeller-core, and some likes the red.
And it's some says "The Little Californy" is the best;
But the sweetest slice of all I ever wedged in my head,
Is the old "Edingburg Mounting-sprout," of the west

You don't want no punkins nigh your wortermelon vines
'Cause, some-way-another, they'll spile your melons, shore;
I've seed 'em taste like punkins, from the core to the rines,
Which may be a fact you have heerd of before

But your melons that's raised right and 'tended to with care,
You can walk around amongst 'em with a parent's pride and joy,
And thump 'em on the heads with as fatherly a air

As ef each one of them was your little girl er boy.

I joy in my hart jest to hear that rippin' sound
When you split one down the back and jolt the halves in two,
And the friends you love the best is gethered all around
And you says unto your sweethart, "Oh, here's the core fer you!"

And I like to slice 'em up in big pieces fer 'em all,
Espeshally the childern, and watch theyr high delight
As one by one the rines with theyr pink notches falls,
And they holler fer some more, with unquenched appetite.

Boys takes to it natchurl, and I like to see 'em eat
A slice of wortermelon's like a frenchharp in theyr hands,
And when they "saw" it through theyr mouth sich music can't be beat
'Cause it's music both the sperit and the stummick understands.

Oh, they's more in wortermelons than the purty-colored meat,
And the overflowin' sweetness of the worter squshed betwixt
The up'ard and the down'ard motions of a feller's teeth,
And it's the taste of ripe old age and juicy childhood mixed.

Fer I never taste a melon but my thoughts flies away
To the summertime of youth; and again I see the dawn,
And the fadin' afternoon of the long summer day,
And the dusk and dew a-fallin', and the night a-comin' on.

And thare's the corn around us, and the lispin' leaves and trees,
And the stars a-peekin' down on us as still as silver mice,
And us boys in the wortermelons on our hands and knees,
And the new-moon hangin' ore us like a yeller-cored slice.

Oh! it's wortermelon time is a-comin' round again,
And they ain't no man a-livin' any tickleder'n me,
Fer the way I hanker after wortermelons is a sin
Which is the why and wharefore, as you can plainly see.

UP AND DOWN OLD BRANDYWINE
Up and down old Brandywine,
In the days 'at's past and gone
With a dad-burn hook-and line
And a saplin' pole, swawn!
I've had more fun, to the square
Inch, than ever ANYwhere!
Heaven to come can't discount MINE
Up and down old Brandywine!

Hain't no sense in WISHIN', yit
Wisht to goodness I COULD jes

"Gee" the blame' world round and git
Back to that old happiness!
Kindo' drive back in the shade
"The old Covered Bridge" there laid
'Crosst the crick, and sorto' soak
My soul over, hub and spoke!

Honest, now! it hain't no DREAM
'At I'm wantin', but THE FAC'S
As they wuz; the same old stream,
And the same old times, i jacks!
Gim me back my bare feet and
Stonebruise too! And scratched and tanned!
And let hottest dog-days shine
Up and down old Brandywine!

In and on betwixt the trees
'Long the banks, pour down yer noon,
Kindo' curdled with the breeze
And the yallerhammer's tune;
And the smokin', chokin' dust
O' the turnpike at its wusst
SATURD'YS, say, when it seems
Road's jes jammed with country teams!

Whilse the old town, fur away
'Crosst the hazy pastur'-land,
Dozed-like in the heat o' day
Peaceful' as a hired hand.
Jolt the gravel th'ough the floor
O' the old bridge! grind and roar
With yer blame percession-line
Up and down old Brandywine!

Souse me and my new straw-hat
Off the foot-log! what I care?
Fist shoved in the crown o' that
Like the old Clown ust to wear.
Wouldn't swop it fer a' old
Gin-u-wine raal crown o' gold!
Keep yer KING ef you'll gim me
Jes the boy I ust to be!

Spill my fishin'-worms! er steal
My best "goggle-eye!" but you
Can't lay hands on joys I feel
Nibblin' like they ust to do!
So, in memory, to-day
Same old ripple lips away
At my "cork" and saggin' line,
Up and down old Bradywine!

There the logs is, round the hill,
Where "Old Irvin" ust to lift
Out sunfish from daylight till
Dewfall 'fore he'd leave "The Drift"
And give US a chance and then
Kindo' fish back home again,
Ketchin' 'em jes left and right
Where WE hadn't got "a bite!"

Er, 'way windin' out and in,
Old path th'ough the iurnweeds
And dog-fennel to yer chin
Then come suddent, th'ough the reeds
And cat-tails, smack into where
Them air woods, hogs ust to scare
Us clean 'crosst the County-line,
Up and down old Brandywine!

But the dim roar o' the dam
It 'ud coax us furder still
To'rds the old race, slow and ca'm,
Slidin' on to Huston's mill
Where, I'spect, "The Freeport crowd"
Never WARMED to us er 'lowed
We wuz quite so overly
Welcome as we aimed to be.

Still it 'peared like ever'thing
Fur away from home as THERE
Had more RELISH-like, i jing!
Fish in stream, er bird in air!
O them rich old bottom-lands,
Past where Cowden's Schoolhouse stands!
Wortermelons MASTER-MINE!
Up and down old Brandywine!

And sich pop-paws! Lumps o' raw
Gold and green, jes oozy th'ough
With ripe yaller like you've saw
Custard-pie with no crust to:
And jes GORGES o' wild plums,
Till a feller'd suck his thumbs
Clean up to his elbows! MY!
ME SOME MORE ER LEM ME DIE!

Up and down old Brandywine!...
Stripe me with pokeberry-juice!
Flick me with a pizenvine
And yell "Yip!" and lem me loose!
Old now as I then wuz young,

'F I could sing as I HAVE sung,
Song 'ud surely ring DEE-VINE
Up and down old Brandywine!

WHEN EARLY MARCH SEEMS MIDDLE MAY
When country roads begin to thaw
In mottled spots of damp and dust,
And fences by the margin draw
Along the frosty crust
Their graphic silhouettes, I say,
The Spring is coming round this way.

When morning-time is bright with sun
And keen with wind, and both confuse
The dancing, glancing eyes of one
With tears that ooze and ooze
And nose-tips weep as well as they,
The Spring is coming round this way.

When suddenly some shadow-bird
Goes wavering beneath the gaze,
And through the hedge the moan is heard
Of kine that fain would graze
In grasses new, I smile and say,
The Spring is coming round this way.

When knotted horse-tails are untied,
And teamsters whistle here and there.
And clumsy mitts are laid aside
And choppers' hands are bare,
And chips are thick where children play,
The Spring is coming round this way.

When through the twigs the farmer tramps,
And troughs are chunked beneath the trees,
And fragrant hints of sugar-camps
Astray in every breeze,
When early March seems middle May,
The Spring is coming round this way.

When coughs are changed to laughs, and when
Our frowns melt into smiles of glee,
And all our blood thaws out again
In streams of ecstasy,
And poets wreak their roundelay,
The Spring is coming round this way.

A TALE OF THE AIRLY DAYS
Oh! tell me a tale of the airly days
Of the times as they ust to be;
"Piller of Fi-er" and "Shakespeare's Plays"
Is a' most too deep fer me!
I want plane facts, and I want plane words,
Of the good old-fashioned ways,
When speech run free as the songs of birds
'Way back in the airly days.

Tell me a tale of the timber-lands
Of the old-time pioneers;
Somepin' a pore man understands
With his feelins's well as ears.
Tell of the old log house, about
The loft, and the puncheon flore
The old fi-er-place, with the crane swung out,
And the latch-string thrugh the door.

Tell of the things jest as they was
They don't need no excuse!
Don't tech 'em up like the poets does,
Tel theyr all too fine fer use!
Say they was 'leven in the fambily
Two beds, and the chist, below,
And the trundle-beds that each helt three,
And the clock and the old bureau.

Then blow the horn at the old back-door
Tel the echoes all halloo,
And the childern gethers home onc't more,
Jest as they ust to do:
Blow fer Pap tel he hears and comes,
With Tomps and Elias, too,
A-marchin' home, with the fife and drums
And the old Red White and Blue!

Blow and blow tel the sound draps low
As the moan of the whipperwill,
And wake up Mother, and Ruth and Jo,
All sleepin' at Bethel Hill:
Blow and call tel the faces all
Shine out in the back-log's blaze,
And the shadders dance on the old hewed wall
As they did in the airly days.

OLD MAN'S NURSERY RHYME
I
In the jolly winters

Of the long-ago,
It was not so cold as now
O! No! No!
Then, as I remember,
Snowballs to eat
Were as good as apples now.
And every bit as sweet!

II

In the jolly winters
Of the dead-and-gone,
Bub was warm as summer,
With his red mitts on,
Just in his little waist-
And-pants all together,
Who ever hear him growl
About cold weather?

III

In the jolly winters
Of the long-ago
Was it HALF so cold as now?
O! No! No!
Who caught his death o' cold,
Making prints of men
Flat-backed in snow that now's
Twice as cold again?

IV

In the jolly winters
Of the dead-and-gone,
Startin' out rabbit-huntin'
Early as the dawn,
Who ever froze his fingers,
Ears, heels, or toes,
Or'd 'a' cared if he had?
Nobody knows!

V

Nights by the kitchen-stove,
Shellin' white and red
Corn in the skillet, and
Sleepin' four abed!
Ah! the jolly winters
Of the long-ago!
We were not as old as now
O! No! No!

JUNE

O queenly month of indolent repose!
I drink thy breath in sips of rare perfume,
As in thy downy lap of clover-bloom
I nestle like a drowsy child and doze
The lazy hours away. The zephyr throws
The shifting shuttle of the Summer's loom
And weaves a damask-work of gleam and gloom
Before thy listless feet. The lily blows
A bugle-call of fragrance o'er the glade;
And, wheeling into ranks, with plume and spear,
Thy harvest-armies gather on parade;
While, faint and far away, yet pure and clear,
A voice calls out of alien lands of shade:
All hail the Peerless Goddess of the Year!

THE TREE-TOAD
"'S cur'ous-like," said the tree-toad,
"I've twittered fer rain all day;
And I got up soon,
And hollered tel noon
But the sun, hit blazed away,
Tell I jest clumb down in a crawfish-hole,
Weary at hart, and sick at soul!

"Dozed away fer an hour,
And I tackled the thing agin:
And I sung, and sung,
Tel I knowed my lung
Was jest about give in;
And THEN, thinks I, ef hit don't rain NOW,
They's nothin' in singin', anyhow!

"Onc't in a while some farmer
Would come a-drivin' past;
And he'd hear my cry,
And stop and sigh
Tel I jest laid back, at last,
And I hollered rain tel I thought my th'oat
Would bust wide open at ever' note!

"But I FETCHED her! O I FETCHED her!
'Cause a little while ago,
As I kindo' set,
With one eye shet,
And a-singin' soft and low,
A voice drapped down on my fevered brain,
A-sayin', 'EF YOU'LL JEST HUSH I'LL RAIN!'"

A SONG OF LONG AGO

A song of Long Ago:
Sing it lightly, sing it low
Sing it softly, like the lisping of the lips we used to know
When our baby-laughter spilled
From the glad hearts ever filled
With music blithe as robin ever trilled!

Let the fragrant summer breeze,
And the leaves of locust-trees,
And the apple-buds and blossoms, and the wings of honey-bees,
All palpitate with glee,
Till the happy harmony
Brings back each childish joy to you and me.

Let the eyes of fancy turn
Where the tumbled pippins burn
Like embers in the orchard's lap of tangled grass and fern,
There let the old path wind
In and out and on behind
The cider-press that chuckles as we grind.

Blend in the song the moan
Of the dove that grieves alone,
And the wild whir of the locust, and the bumble's drowsy drone;
And the low of cows that call
Through the pasture-bars when all
The landscape fades away at evenfall.

Then, far away and clear,
Through the dusky atmosphere,
Let the wailing of the killdee be the only sound we hear:
O sad and sweet and low
As the memory may know
Is the glad-pathetic song of Long Ago!

OLD WINTERS ON THE FARM

I have jest about decided
It 'ud keep a town-boy hoppin'
Fer to work all winter, choppin'
Fer a' old fireplace, like I did!
Lawz! them old times wuz contrairy!
Blame' backbone o' winter, 'peared-like

WOULDN'T break! and I wuz skeered-like
Clean on into FEB'UARY!
Nothin' ever made me madder
Than fer Pap to stomp in, layin'
In a' extra forestick, say'in',
"Groun'-hog's out and seed his shadder!"

ROMANCIN'
I' b'en a-kindo' "musin'," as the feller says, and I'm
About o' the conclusion that they hain't no better time,
When you come to cipher on it, than the times we ust to know
When we swore our first "dog-gone-it" sorto' solum-like and low!

You git my idy, do you? LITTLE tads, you understand
Jest a-wishin' thue and thue you that you on'y wuz a MAN.
Yit here I am, this minit, even sixty, to a day,
And fergittin' all that's in it, wishm' jest the other way!

I hain't no hand to lectur' on the times, er dimonstrate
Whare the trouble is, er hector and domineer with Fate,
But when I git so flurried, and so pestered-like and blue,
And so rail owdacious worried, let me tell you what I do!

I jest gee-haw the hosses, and onhook the swingle-tree,
Whare the hazel-bushes tosses down theyr shadders over me;
And I draw my plug o' navy, and I climb the fence, and set
Jest a-thinkin' here, i gravy' tel my eyes is wringin'-wet!

Tho' I still kin see the trouble o' the PRESUNT, I kin see
Kindo' like my sight wuz double-all the things that UST to be;
And the flutter o' the robin and the teeter o' the wren
Sets the willer-branches bobbin' "howdy-do" thum Now to Then!

The deadnin' and the thicket's jest a-bilin' full of June,
From the rattle o' the cricket, to the yallar-hammer's tune;
And the catbird in the bottom, and the sapsuck on the snag,
Seems ef they can't-od-rot 'em!-jest do nothin' else but brag!

They's music in the twitter of the bluebird and the jay,
And that sassy little critter jest a-peckin' all the day;
They's music in the "flicker," and they's music in the thrush,
And they's music in the snicker o' the chipmunk in the brush!

They's music all around me! And I go back, in a dream
Sweeter yit than ever found me fast asleep, and in the stream
That list to split the medder whare the dandylions growed,
I stand knee-deep, and redder than the sunset down the road.

Then's when I' b'en a-fishin'! And they's other fellers, too,

With theyr hick'ry-poles a-swishin' out behind 'em; and a few
Little "shiners" on our stringers, with theyr tails tip toein' bloom,
As we dance 'em in our fingers all the happy jurney home.

I kin see us, true to Natur', thum the time we started out,
With a biscuit and a 'tater in our little "roundabout"!
I kin see our lines a-tanglin', and our elbows in a jam,
And our naked legs a-danglin' thum the apern o' the dam.

I kin see the honeysuckle climbin' up around the mill,
And kin hear the worter chuckle, and the wheel a-growlin' still;
And thum the bank below it I kin steal the old canoe,
And jest git in and row it like the miller ust to do.

W'y, I git my fancy focussed on the past so mortul plane
I kin even smell the locus'-blossoms bloomin' in the lane;
And I hear the cow-bells clinkin' sweeter tunes 'n "Money-musk"'
Fer the lightnin' bugs a-blinkin' and a-dancin' in the dusk.

And when I've kep' on "musin'," as the feller says, tel I'm
Firm-fixed in the conclusion that they haint no better time,
When you come to cipher on it, than the old times, I de-clare
I kin wake and say "dog-gone-it'" jest as soft as any prayer!

James Whitcomb Riley – A Short Biography

Poet and author James Whitcomb Riley was born on October 7th 1849 in Greenfield, Indiana. Known as the "Hoosier Poet" for his work with regional dialects, and as the "Children's Poet" for his children's poetry and devotion to youth causes, Riley is best remembered as the author of the well-loved verse book, *Rhymes of Childhood*.

Riley grew up in a well-off and influential family. Riley's father, Reuben Andrew Riley, was a lawyer and Democrat member of the Indiana House of Representatives and he named his son for his friend James Whitcomb, then the governor of Indiana.

Riley had a spotty education, learning at home and attending his local school sporadically (he did not graduate Grade 8 until the age of twenty). Nonetheless, his was a childhood full of creativity. He learned about poetry from an uncle who was a poet and enthusiast and was encouraged by his mother to write and produce juvenile theatrical presentations. His father taught him how to play the guitar and Riley went on to perform in a local band.

Life changed when Riley's father went off to fight in the Civil War in 1861. The family (which already included six children) took in an additional orphan child and suffered many hardships. Riley would base his famous poem, *Little Orphant Annie* on this temporary foster sibling (both the child and the poem were named "Allie", but a typesetter made a crucial typo when the poem was finally published).

Riley Senior returned from soldiering a broken man, partially paralyzed and unable to resume his practice. The family was forced to sell their house in town and retreated to the family farm where

Riley's mother died in 1870. Riley became estranged from his father at this time and left home. He also started drinking excessively, beginning a life-long habit that would both impact his health and his career.

He embarked on a series of low-paying jobs – house painting, Bible salesman – before starting a sign-painting business in Greenfield. Riley wrote catchy slogans for his signs, in effect, his first published verses. He also started participating in local theatre productions and sending poems to the *Indianapolis Mirror* under the pseudonym "Jay Whit".

When he went to work for the McGrillus Company in Anderson, Indiana shilling tonic medicines in a travelling show that visited small towns around the state, he discovered another calling. Riley both wrote and performed skits promoting the tonics. Eventually, Riley and several friends started a billboard company that became successful enough that he was able to turn to writing in a more committed way, and he returned to Greenfield to do so.

Riley started sending out dozens of poems to newspapers around the country and many of them – the *Danbury News*, the *Indianapolis Journal* and the *Anderson Democrat*, among them – published the verses. At the same time, Riley began to write to prominent American writers, sending poems and requesting their endorsement. He was successful with poet Henry Wadsworth Longfellow who wrote back, "I have read the poems with great pleasure, and I think they show a true poetic faculty and insight." Riley would finally meet Longfellow in person shortly before the latter's death in 1882; he famously wrote about the experience and about Longfellow's profound impact on his work.

The *Anderson Democrat* offered Riley a reporting job in 1877. He took it on while continuing to submit poems at journals and newspapers all over the country. Riley would lose the stability of this reporting job when a prank in which he submitted a poem to a journal claiming it was Edgar Allan Poe's went awry. Spurned by many publishers after this embarrassing incident, Riley joined a travelling lecture circuit and gave poetry readings around the state. A born entertainer, Riley's readings would become hugely popular and remained a primary source of income for most of his life.

Eventually, the Poe debacle faded into the background and the *Indianapolis Journal* relented, hiring Riley as a columnist in 1879; he wrote regularly for them about society affairs while continuing to tour his increasingly theatrical and comedic poetry readings. As his fame increased, Riley dropped his "Jay Whit" pseudonym and wrote under his own name from about 1881.

Around this time Riley began writing what are known as his "Boone County poems". They are almost entirely written in dialect and emphasize rural and agricultural topics, often evoking nostalgia for the simplicity of country life. *The Old Swimmin'-Hole* and *When the Frost Is on the Punkin'* were the most popular, and helped earn the entire series critical acclaim. In 1883, a friend arranged for the private publication of *The Old Swimmin' Hole and 'Leven More Poems'*. The book's popularity dictated a second printing before the end of the year and it continued to sell for years, bolstered by Riley's reading tours.

Riley's prose style lent itself well to public performance. With their emphasis on the natural speech rhythms of mid-western dialects, his most famous poems – *Raggedy Man*, *Little Orphant Annie* – can look slightly ridiculous on the page. But they come alive when read aloud:

Little Orphant Annie's come to our house to stay,
An' wash the cups an' saucers up, an' brush the crumbs away,
An' shoo the chickens off the porch, an' dust the hearth, an'sweep,

An' make the fire, an' bake the bread, an' earn her board-an'-keep;
An' all us other childern, when the supper-things is done,
We set around the kitchen fire an' has the mostest fun
A-list'nin' to the witch-tales 'at Annie tells about,
An' the Gobble-uns 'at gits you
Ef you
Don't
Watch
Out!

This phenomenon is likely the key to Riley's success with children's verse, as well as the reason he was able to build such fame and fortune on the travelling lecture circuit. It helped also that he was a confident and talented performer.

In 1881 Riley was invited to tour with the Redpath Lyceum Circuit, a prominent series that included writers such as Ralph Waldo Emerson on its roster of regular lecturers. After a successful first season reading in Chicago and Indianapolis, Riley signed a ten-year contract with the Circuit and embarked on a tour of the Eastern seaboard starting in Boston. Riley toured with the Circuit until 1885 when he joined forces with humourist Edgar Wilson Nye. In 1888, the pair co-wrote *Nye and Riley's Railway Guide*, a collection of poems and anecdotes. Nye and Riley also teamed up with another famous American humourist Samuel Clemons (Mark Twain) for joint performances in New York City. Despite contract and agent woes that deprived Riley of his full share of the proceeds, he continued touring with Nye through 1890.

Riley published his third compilation of work in 1888. *Old-Fashioned Roses* was written specifically for the British market and consisted mostly of sonnets; Riley intentionally left his country bumpkin dialects out of this collection. The book was a predictable success in the UK and Riley travelled to Scotland (where he made a pilgrimage to the grave of Robert Burns, a poet with who he is often compared) and England to promote it and conduct readings in 1891.

Back home the next year Riley resumed his lecture and reading tour, teaming up with millionaire author Douglass Sherley for a hugely successful double bill. Coinciding with this, in a savvy and astute cross-promotion, Riley compiled and published perhaps his best-loved book, *Rhymes of Childhood*. It's a work that continues to be popular into the 21st century. It also parted the beginning of the end for Riley's literary reputation. Although he continued to sell out readings in New York and across the US (in fact prospective audience members were often turned away), critics increasingly found his work repetitive and banal. His 1894 verse volume *Armazindy* was very poorly received.

Riley gave his last tour in 1895 and spent his final years in Indianapolis writing patriotic poetry for public recitation on civic occasions (with stirring titles such as *America!* and *The Name of Old Glory*) and poem/elegies for famous friends. His life's work of essays, poems, plays and articles was published in sixteen volumes in 1914.

By this time, Riley was in poor health, weakened by years of heavy drinking. The Hoosier Poet died on July 23, 1916 of a stroke. In a final, unusual tribute, Riley lay in state for a day in the Indiana Statehouse, where thousands came to pay their respects. Not since Lincoln had a public personage received such a send-off. He is buried at Crown Hill Cemetery in Indianapolis.

Riley's legacy is not just a literary one. A wealthy man, he left behind the funding seeds for a number of memorial projects, the James Whitcomb Riley Hospital for Children, Camp Riley for children with disabilities and James Whitcomb Riley House (a museum in which the writer's personal effects and furnishings from his lifetime remain unchanged).

And, as a lasting tribute, the town of Greenfield holds a festival every year in Riley's honor. Every October the "Riley Days" festival opens with a flower parade in which local school children place flowers around the statue of Riley set on the courthouse lawn.

Remembered as both a philanthropist and a poet laureate for the Hoosier state of Indiana, a writer with a distinctive pre-industrial folk ethos and an ear for the humble rhythms of the plain local dialect of the US Midwest, Riley remains to this day a poet of the people.

www.ingramcontent.com/pod-product-compliance
Lightning Source LLC
Chambersburg PA
CBHW071413040426
42444CB00009B/2230